WHAT WE DO NOW

WHAT WE DO NOW

STANDING UP FOR YOUR VALUES IN TRUMP'S AMERICA

EDITED BY DENNIS JOHNSON
AND VALERIE MERIANS

 MELVILLE HOUSE

BROOKLYN • LONDON

WHAT WE DO NOW

Melville House Publishing
46 John Street   and
Brooklyn, NY 11201

8 Blackstock Mews
Islington
London N4 2BT

mhpbooks.com   facebook.com/mhpbooks   @melvillehouse

Design by Wah-Ming Chang

ISBN: 978-1-61219-659-6

Printed in the United States of America
1   3   5   7   9   10   8   6   4   2

A catalog record for this book is available
from the Library of Congress

CONTENTS

INTRODUCTION

BY DENNIS JOHNSON

Somehow, the United States has always averted a takeover from the far right. It was something that made our country great. From Father Coughlan and the fascists of the 1920s and '30s, to Joe McCarthy and the Cold War demagoguery of the 1940s and '50s, through George Wallace and the white supremacists of the 1960s, and on, Americans have always, ultimately, resisted the call to calamity by listening, instead, to what Lincoln called "the better angels of our nature."

It was such a long spell—nearly a century—that we were all perhaps too secure in the idea that "it can't happen here."

But now it has. It has happened here. The most extreme and uncouth right-wing candidate ever to run for high office in the United States has somehow won the presidency. No one in the long history of American politics has ever so openly attacked the rich demographics of this nation, formed, after all, from its inception by immigrants—crude attack after attack upon women, Hispanics, African Americans, the disabled, Muslims, and Jews—while also impugning the idea of a free press. It's important to note that the demagogues being cited in comparison—Donald Trump quoted Mussolini on the campaign trail—were also considered buffoons at first, mocked for their appearance. A weird little mustache, a shaved head with jackboots, a bizarrely bright orange hairstyle . . .

It has happened here.

The despair at this is widespread and lingering, and is abetted by the fact that, well, significantly more people—millions, in fact—voted for the woman who somehow lost the election.

Which is to say that the grief—for that's what it is—is earned. It is an unprecedented development in the history of our democracy, and one that seems indeed to spell doom for that democracy. How can the defeated majority rouse itself to overcome its sincere grief and disillusionment?

These twenty-seven essays by some of the best and the brightest of America's progressive leaders—hereby announcing themselves as the new American resistance movement—offer some galvanizing answers. They suggest actual strategies on how to move forward in the face of what seem to be overwhelming odds. And beyond the practical, they offer something else—the notion that we who are appalled by this are not alone, and can do something about it if we join forces.

To be sure, it will be a long struggle—four years at least, we have to presume—and difficult. Very difficult. But now is indeed the time for all good people to come to the aid of their country, and its founding and inclusive principles of democracy—in short, to actually make America great again.

WHAT
WE DO
NOW

I

SETTING A NEW LIBERAL AGENDA

WHERE DO WE GO FROM HERE?

Bernie Sanders

Bernie Sanders is the junior U.S. senator from Vermont.

WHERE DO WE GO FROM HERE?

The time is long overdue for real financial reform in this country. It will not be easy given the enormous power of Wall Street and its political supporters, but it is absolutely necessary if we are to have the kind of strong and stable economy that we need to rebuild the shrinking middle class.

The "heads, bankers win/tails, everyone else loses" system must come to an end. We need to create a financial system that works for ordinary Americans, not just those on top. Here are just some of the steps forward that will help us achieve that goal.

ENDING "TOO BIG TO FAIL"

To create an economy that works for all Americans and not just a handful of billionaires, we have got to address the ever-increasing size of the mega-banks. And we must end, once and for all, the scheme that is nothing more than a free insurance policy for Wall Street: the policy of "too big to fail."

We need a banking system that is part of a productive economy—making loans at affordable rates to small- and medium-size businesses so that we create a growing economy with decent-paying jobs. We need a banking system that encourages homeownership by offering affordable mortgage products that are designed to work for both the lender and the borrower. We need a banking system that is transparent and accountable, and that adheres to the highest ethical standards as well as to the spirit and the letter of the law.

This is not the banking system we have today. Wall Street cannot continue to be an island unto itself, gambling trillions of other people's dollars on risky derivatives, acting illegally, and making huge profits, all the while assured that if its schemes fail, the taxpayers will be there to bail them out.

Of course, that is precisely what happened in 2008, when taxpayers bailed out Wall Street. Financial institutions received a $700 billion gift from Congress. And, thanks to an amendment I offered in 2010, we were able to learn that the Federal Reserve provided $16 trillion in secret loans to some of the largest financial institutions and corporations in the United States and throughout the world. We were told that these unprecedented actions were necessary because the financial institutions involved were simply "too big to fail." In other words, they were so large and intertwined with all aspects of the economy that if they collapsed, the U.S. economy and maybe the entire global economy would go down with them.

One might have thought, as part of the bailout, these huge banks would have been reduced in size to make certain that we never experience a recurrence of what happened in 2008. Well, that's not exactly what happened. In fact, the very opposite occurred. Today, three out of the four largest financial institutions—JPMorgan Chase, Bank of America, and Wells Fargo—are about 80 percent bigger than they were before we bailed them out.

Today the six largest banks issue more than two-thirds of all credit cards and more than 35 percent of all mortgages. They control more than 95 percent of financial derivatives and hold more than 40 percent of all bank deposits. Their assets have almost quadrupled since the mid-1990s and are now equivalent to nearly 60 percent of our GDP.

If these banks were too big to fail in 2008, what would happen if any of them were to fail today? The taxpayers would be on the hook again, and almost certainly for more money than in the last bailout. We cannot allow that to happen. No financial institution should be so large that its failure would cause catastrophic risk to millions of Americans or to our nation's economic well-being. No financial institution should have holdings so extensive that its failure would send the world economy into crisis.

If a bank is too big to fail, it is too big to exist. When it comes to Wall Street reform, that must be our bottom line. This is true not just because of the risk to the economy of another collapse and another bailout; it is also true because the current extreme concentration of ownership in the financial industry allows a very small number of huge financial institutions to have far too much economic and political power over this country.

If Teddy Roosevelt, the Republican trustbuster, were alive today, he would say, "Break 'em up." And he would be right.

Here's how we can do it.

We must pass legislation to cap the size of the largest financial institutions in this country so that their assets are no more than 2 percent of GDP—which is equal to about $350 billion today. This would break up the ten biggest banks in the country: JPMorgan Chase, Bank of America, Citigroup, Wells Fargo, Goldman Sachs, Morgan Stanley, U.S. Bancorp, PNC, Bank of New York Mellon, and HSBC North America.

This is not a radical idea. Under this plan, the size of JPMorgan Chase would simply go back to where it was in 1997; Bank of America would shrink to where it was in 1998; Wells Fargo would return to where it was in 2002; and Citigroup would shrink to where it was during the second term of Bill Clinton's administration.

Breaking up the big banks would reduce systemic risk in our financial system. It would also mean increased competition. Oligopolies—where the market is dominated by just a few economic actors—are never good for consumers. Smaller banks are more likely to offer affordable financial products that Americans actually want and need, and consumers would have more banking products to choose from.

The idea of breaking up the too-big-to-fail banks is supported not only by a number of progressive economists, but also by some leading figures in the financial community.

The Independent Community Bankers of America, representing six thousand community banks, supports the idea because they understand that the function of banking should not be about speculation in derivatives and other esoteric financial instruments. Rather, it should be about providing affordable loans to businesses to create jobs in a productive economy, and providing Americans with loans they can afford to purchase homes, cars, and other consumer needs.

In other worlds, the function of banking should be boring.

Past and present presidents of Federal Reserve banks in Dallas, St. Louis, Kansas City, and Minneapolis also support breaking up these behemoth banks. While these individuals are much more conservative than I am, all of them understand how dangerous too-big-to-fail banks are to our economy.

And I am proud that for the first time, the Democratic Party is on record as supporting this concept as well, thanks to an agreement our campaign worked out with Hillary Clinton's campaign. The 2016 Democratic National Committee platform declares: "Banks should not be able to gamble with taxpayers' deposits or pose an undue risk to Main Street. Democrats support a variety of ways to stop this from happening, including . . . breaking up too-big-to-fail financial institutions that pose a systemic risk to the stability of our economy."

This is a very important political step forward. Now it is our job to make sure the next president and Congress turn that platform statement into reality.

REMARKS TO THE AFL-CIO EXECUTIVE COUNCIL

Elizabeth Warren

Elizabeth Warren is the senior U.S. senator from Massachusetts.

Delivered in Washington, D.C., on November 10, 2016.

We are now two days removed from an incredibly close and hard-fought election, and many people here in Washington and all across the country are trying to make sense of what happened.

This wasn't a pretty election. In fact, it was ugly, and we should not sugarcoat why. Donald Trump ran a campaign that started with racial attacks and then he rode the escalator down. He encouraged a toxic stew of hatred and fear. He attacked millions of Americans. He regularly made statements that undermined core values of our democracy.

And he won. He won—and now Latino and Muslim-American children are worried about what will happen to their families. LGBT couples are worried that their marriages could be dissolved by a Trump-Pence Supreme Court. Women are worried that access to desperately needed health services will disappear. Millions of people in this country are worried. And they are right to be worried.

Today, as president-elect, Donald Trump has an opportunity to chart a different course: to govern for all Americans and to respect our institutions. In his victory speech, he pledged that he would be "president for all" of the American people. And when he takes the oath of office as the leader of our democracy and leader of all Americans, I sincerely hope that he will fulfill that pledge with respect and concern for every single human being in this country, no matter who they are, no matter where they come from, no matter what they believe, no matter whom they love.

And that marks Democrats' first job in this new era: We will stand up to bigotry. No compromises ever on this one. Bigotry in all its forms: we will fight back against attacks on Latinos, on African Americans, on women, on Muslims, on immigrants, on disabled Americans—on anyone. Whether Donald Trump sits in a glass tower or sits in the White House, we will not give an inch on this, not now, not ever.

But let's be clear on this point. There are many millions of people who voted for Donald Trump not because of the bigotry and hate that fueled his campaign rallies. They voted for him despite the hate. They voted for him out of frustration and anger—and out of hope that he would make real change in this country.

If we have learned nothing else from the past two years of electioneering, we should hear the message loud and clear that the American people want Washington to change. It was clear in the Democratic primaries. It was clear in the Republican primaries. It was clear in the campaign and it was clear on Election Day. The final results may have divided us—but the entire electorate embraced deep, fundamental reform of our economic system and our political system.

Working families across this country are deeply frustrated about an economy and a government that doesn't work for them. Exit polling on Tuesday found that 72 percent of voters believe that, quote, "the American economy is rigged to advantage the rich and powerful." That's 72 percent of *all* voters—Democrats and Republicans. The polls also made clear that the economy was the top issue on voters' minds . . . voters who are angry about a federal government that works for the rich and powerful and that leaves everyone else behind.

Lobbyists and Washington insiders have spent years trying to convince themselves and each other that Americans don't actually believe this. And now that the returns are in and the people have spoken, they're already trying to wave their hands and dismiss these views as some sort of mass delusion. Well they are wrong—they are very wrong.

The truth is that people are right to be angry. Angry that wages have been stagnant for a generation, while basic costs like housing, health care, and child care have skyrocketed. Angry that our political system is awash in barely legalized campaign bribery. Angry that Washington eagerly protects the tax breaks for billionaires while it refuses to raise the minimum wage, or help millions of Americans struggling with student loans, or enforce the law when the millionaire CEOs who fund our political campaigns break it. Angry that Washington pushes big corporate interests in trade deals, but won't make the investments in infrastructure to create good jobs right here in America. Angry that Washington tilts the playing field for giant corporations—giving them special privileges, and letting them amass enormous economic and political power.

Angry that while Washington dithers and spins and does the backstroke in an ocean of money, the American Dream moves further and further out of reach for most families. Angry that working people are in debt. Angry that seniors can't stretch a Social Security check to cover the basics.

President-elect Trump spoke to these issues. Republican elites hated him for it. But he didn't care. He did it anyway. He criticized Wall Street and big money's dominance in Washington—straight up. He supported a new Glass-Steagall. He spoke of the need to reform our trade deals so they aren't a raw deal for the American people. He said he will not cut Social Security benefits. He talked about the need to address the rising cost of college and about helping working parents struggling with the high cost of child care. He spoke of the urgency of rebuilding our crumbling infrastructure and putting people back to work. He spoke to the very real sense millions of Americans have that their government and their economy has abandoned them. And he promised to rebuild this economy for working people.

The deep worry that people feel over an America that does not work for them is not a liberal or a conservative worry. It is not a Democratic or a Republican worry. It is the deep worry that led even Americans with deep reservations about Donald Trump's temperament and fitness to vote for him anyway.

So let me be 100 percent clear about this. When President-elect Trump wants to take on these issues, when his goal is to increase the economic security of middle-class families, then count me in. I will push aside our differences and I will work with him to achieve that goal. I offer to work as hard as I can and to pull as many people as I can into this effort. If Trump is ready to go on rebuilding American economic security for millions of families, then I am ready and so are a lot of other people—Democrats and Republicans.

But let me also be clear about what rebuilding our economy does not mean.

It does not mean handing the keys to our economy over to Wall Street so they can run it for themselves. Americans want to hold the big banks accountable. That will not happen if we gut Dodd-Frank and fire the cops responsible for watching over those banks, like the Consumer Financial Protection Bureau. If Trump and the Republican Party try to turn loose the big banks and financial institutions so they can once again gamble with our economy and bring it all crashing down, then we will fight them every step of the way. Every step.

And rebuilding our economy does not mean crippling our economy and ripping working families apart by rounding up and deporting millions of our coworkers, our friends and our neighbors, our mothers and our fathers, our sons and our daughters. If Republicans choose that path, we will fight them every step of the way.

And health care. Americans want reform to Obama-care—Democrats included. We must bring down the costs of health insurance and the cost of health care overall. But if the Republicans want to strip away health insurance from 20 million Americans, if they want to let cancer survivors get kicked to the curb, if they want to throw twenty-four-year-olds off their parents' health insurance, then we will fight them every step of the way.

Americans want to close tax loopholes that benefit the very rich; Donald Trump claimed to support closing the carried interest loophole and other loopholes as well. We need a fairer tax system, but if Republicans want to force through massive tax breaks that blow a hole in our deficit and tilt the playing field even further toward the wealthy and big corporations, then we will fight them every step of the way.

The American people—Democrats, Republicans, and Independents—have been clear about what economic policies they want Washington to pursue. Two-thirds of the people in this country support raising the federal minimum wage. Three-quarters of Americans want the federal government to increase its infrastructure investments. Over 70 percent of Americans believe students should have a chance at a debt-free college. Nearly three-quarters support expanding Social Security. These are the kinds of policies that will help level the playing field for working families and address the frustrations felt by millions of people across the country.

This is an American agenda.

You know, the American people sent one more message as well. Economic reform requires political reform. Why has the government worked so long for only those at the top? The answer is money—money—and the American people want this system changed. The American people are sick of politicians wallowing in campaign contributions and dark money. They are revolted by influence peddling by wealthy people and giant corporations. Keep in mind, when Bernie Sanders proved his independence by running a campaign based on small-dollar contributions, and when Donald Trump promised to spend his own money on his campaign, both were sending the important message that they could not be bought. And once again, if Donald Trump is ready to make good on his promise to get corruption out of politics, to end dark money and pay-to-play, then count me in. I will work as hard as I can. I will pull as many people as I can into the fight to end the influence of big money and return democracy to the people. That's what I believe.

Donald Trump won the presidency under a Republican flag, but Mitch McConnell, Paul Ryan, and the Republicans in Congress—and their way of doing business—were rejected: rejected by their own primary voters, rejected during the campaign, and rejected in Tuesday's election. Regardless of political party, working families are disgusted by a Washington that works for the rich and powerful and leaves everyone else behind.

The American people have called out loudly for economic and political reform. For years, too many Republicans and too many Democrats have refused to hear their demands.

The majority of Americans voted against Donald Trump. Democrats picked up seats in both the House and the Senate. And yet, here we are. Republicans are in control of both houses of Congress and the White House. And that makes our job clear. As the loyal opposition we will fight harder, we will fight longer, and we will fight more passionately than ever for the rights of every human being in this country to be treated with respect and dignity. We will fight for economic opportunity, not just for some of our kids, but for all of our kids. We do not control the tools of government, but make no mistake, we know what we stand for, the sun will keep rising, and we will keep fighting—each day, every day, we will fight for the people of this country. That's what we will do.

The time for ignoring the American people is over. It is time for us to come together to work on America's agenda. Democracy demands that we do so, and we are ready.

THE WAY TO STOP TRUMP

David Cole

David Cole is the national legal director of the American Civil Liberties Union (ACLU).

The stunning upset election of Donald Trump has left many Americans wondering what has become of their country, their party, their government, even their sense of the world. Purple prose has been unleashed on the problem; comparisons to fascism and totalitarianism abound. Commentators claim that Trump's election reflects a racist, sexist, xenophobic America. But we should resist the temptation to draw broad-brush generalizations about American character from the election's outcome. The result was far more equivocal than that; a majority of the voters rejected Trump, after all. There is no question that President Trump will be a disaster—if we let him. But the more important point is that—as the fate of American democracy in the years after 9/11 has taught us—we can and must stop him.

The risks are almost certainly greater than those posed by any prior American president. Trump, who has no government experience, a notoriously unreliable temperament, and a record of demagoguery and lies, will come to office with Republican majorities in both houses of Congress, and, once he fills the late Antonin Scalia's seat, on the Supreme Court as well. His shortlist of cabinet appointees offers little hope that voices of moderation will be heard.

Who, then, is going to stop him? Will he be able to put in place all the worst ideas he tossed out so cavalierly on the campaign trail? Building a wall; banning and deporting Muslims; ending Obamacare; reneging on climate change treaty responsibilities; expanding libel law; criminalizing abortion; jailing his political opponents; supporting aggressive stop-and-frisk policing; reviving mass surveillance and torture?

Whether Trump will actually try to implement these promises, and more importantly, whether he will succeed if he does try, lies as much in our hands as in his. If Americans let him, Trump may well do all that he promised—and more. Imagine, for example, what a Trump administration might do if there is another serious terrorist attack on U.S. soil. What little he has said about national security suggests that he will make us nostalgic for George W. Bush and Dick Cheney.

We let a minority of voters give Trump the presidency by not turning out to vote for Clinton (Trump didn't even get as many votes as McCain and Romney, but Clinton received nearly 5 million fewer votes than Obama in 2012). But if we now and for the next four years insist that he honor our most fundamental constitutional values, including equality, human dignity, fair process, privacy, and the rule of law, and if we organize and advocate in defense of those principles, he can and will be contained. It won't happen overnight. There will be many protracted struggles. The important thing to bear in mind is that if we fight, we can prevail.

If you think this is overly naive, consider the fate of George Bush's "war on terror." In the immediate aftermath of the terrorist attacks of September 11, 2001, Bush acted as if he were entirely unconstrained. He had reason to think that he could get away with it. His popularity soared to its highest level. The Supreme Court had just voted to put him in office. He had a solid Republican majority in the House of Representatives, and the Democrats had only a razor-thin majority in the Senate (thanks to Senator James Jeffords's decision in June 2001 to switch from Republican to Independent and to caucus with the Democrats).

More to the point, history was on Bush's side: neither Congress, the Supreme Court, nor the American people had ever put up much, if any, resistance to a president in dealing with the "enemy" in a time of war. Presidents had jailed hundreds for merely speaking out against the war in World War I, and had interned 110,000 people on the basis of their Japanese ancestry during World War II. We and our institutions did nothing to stop those efforts. Assuming he would have a similarly free hand, Bush authorized disappearances of terror suspects into secret CIA prisons, torture as an interrogation tactic, indefinite detention at Guantanamo without hearing or judicial review, "extraordinary rendition" of suspects to third countries so that they could torture them for us, and warrantless electronic surveillance of Americans. He insisted that he could ignore federal criminal statutes, that the Geneva Conventions did not apply to al-Qaeda detainees, and that Guantanamo was beyond the law.

For much of his first term, Bush did indeed get away with such tactics. But much to his dismay, Americans did not sit back and accept that the executive was above the law. As I describe in my recent book, *Engines of Liberty: The Power of Citizen Activists to Make Constitutional Law*, they protested, filed lawsuits, wrote human rights reports, lobbied foreign audiences and governments to bring pressure to bear on the United States, leaked classified documents, and broadly condemned the administration's actions as violations of fundamental constitutional and human rights. Human Rights First organized retired generals and admirals; the Center for Constitutional Rights and Reprieve, aided by an army of pro bono lawyers, brought the plight of Guantanamo detainees to the world's attention; the Bill of Rights Defense Committee sparked a grassroots protest through local referenda on the Patriot Act; and the ACLU used the Freedom of Information Act to dislodge thousands of documents detailing the CIA's torture program, which it and PEN American Center then disseminated in accessible form. The academy, the press, and the international community all joined in the condemnation.

As a result, the course of history changed. By the time Bush left office in 2009, he had released more than five hundred of the detainees from Guantanamo, emptied out the CIA's secret prisons, halted the CIA interrogation program and extraordinary renditions, and placed the NSA's surveillance program under judicial supervision. His claims of uncheckable executive power had been rejected; the Geneva Conventions applied to all detainees.

Bush did not introduce these reforms because he came to realize his wrongs. His memoir, like that of his vice president, Dick Cheney, is entirely unrepentant. But Bush was nonetheless checked—by American civil society, international criticism, and, for the first time in history, the Court and Congress. The Supreme Court established that any detainee held at Guantanamo has a right to judicial review (*Boumediene v. Bush*), that the Geneva Conventions apply to all al-Qaeda detainees (*Hamdan v. Rumsfeld*), and that the president cannot hold U.S. citizens as enemy combatants without affording them a meaningful opportunity to defend themselves (*Hamdi v. Rumsfeld*).

In 2005, Congress—under Republican Senator John McCain's leadership and over the administration's strenuous objections—adopted the Detainee Treatment Act, a bipartisan prohibition on the use of cruel, inhuman, and degrading tactics against anyone in U.S. custody—therefore barring waterboarding and other patently cruel interrogation techniques.

These rules and precedents will rein in Trump, just as they reined in Bush. Moreover, the combined effect of international condemnation of the CIA torture program, Obama's repudiation of it, and the damning report about it by the Senate Select Committee on Intelligence will make any effort to revive those tactics extraordinarily difficult. (By contrast, Obama's troubling use of drones to engage in secret targeted killing far from any battlefield leaves Trump an extremely dangerous weapon. While Obama introduced some reforms to the drone program in the latter part of his administration, they are not binding on a subsequent president, and because the existing guidelines

continue to permit secret killing, they defeat any meaningful accountability.)

So if Bush could be stopped, notwithstanding widespread popular support, a large-scale attack on U.S. soil
leading to war footing, and a history of judicial and con-
gressional acquiescence in similar periods, Trump is also
stoppable. He doesn't have anything like the popular support Bush had after 9/11. And the recent history of the repudiation of Bush's abuses will make it harder to repeat them.

Much of what Trump has proposed is patently illegal.
Torture violates the Constitution, international law, and the
Geneva Conventions. Deporting or singling out Muslims for
discriminatory treatment violates religious freedom. Congress cannot expand libel, whose contours are determined
by the First Amendment. The right to terminate a pregnancy
remains protected by the Constitution, and the Supreme
Court strongly reaffirmed that right just last year. A bipartisan Congress ended the NSA's bulk collection of Americans'
phone metadata in 2015, after a court of appeals ruled the
program illegal. And the terms of our climate change treaty
preclude backing out for four years.

There is no way to guarantee that Trump will not try to
implement at least some of his campaign promises. He has
already vowed to deport 2 to 3 million people, and to repeal
and replace major parts of Obamacare. The time to stop him
in his tracks was at the voting booth, and we failed to do
that. But as the fate of the Bush administration's counter-
terror measures illustrates, even when the executive seems
most invincible, he can be checked. Doing so will take an
engaged citizenry, a persistent civil society, a vigilant media,
brave insiders, and judges and other government officials

who take seriously their responsibility to uphold the Constitution. (I look forward to taking part in this effort myself as National Legal Director of the ACLU, effective a few days before Trump takes office.)

We live in a constitutional democracy, one that is expressly designed to check the impulses of dangerous men. It will do so if and only if we insist on it.

2

RACIAL JUSTICE

EVOLVING TRUMP'S AMERICA INTO THE OTHER AMERICA WE LOVE

Cornell William Brooks

Cornell William Brooks is the president and CEO of the National Association for the Advancement of Colored People (NAACP).

The election of Donald Trump as the nation's forty-fifth president represents a radical moment of awakening for not only people of color, but the American majority. In the final tally, more than 2 million more Americans voted against his abrasive rhetoric than for it. Despite this, he, instead of Hillary Clinton, will be the one setting our nation's political agenda for the next four years.

During this election, bigotry resurfaced in ways we assumed were no longer relevant, and racism was normalized. The xenophobic and divisive rhetoric espoused has unsurprisingly formed a polluted watering hole for many who thirst for ways to demonize other Americans.

The most recent FBI report on hate crimes showed a 6 percent increase in hate crime incidents reported to the police in 2015, including a 67 percent rise in anti-Muslim hate crimes.

Since the election, the Southern Poverty Law Center has received reports of more than 437 hate crimes—equal to 7.5 percent of all the hate crime incidents reported to the FBI in all of 2015. In North Carolina, on the heels of multiple court decisions calling out the intentional disenfranchisement of black voters, one vandalized building proclaimed, "Black lives doesn't matter and neither does your vote."

These are the dangerous, tangible consequences of the eloquent articulation of fear.

In a sense, many of Trump's ideals represent an America that is not ours. His America is an America where the system is "rigged," while past and present oppression is brushed away as irrelevant.

His America is not always our America, yet our connection remains, like the West African Adinkra symbol of an alligator with two heads: it represents unity in diversity and a shared destiny. We can no more ignore him and those he represents than he can frighten our nation away from the progressive ideals of freedom, justice, and inclusion.

Despite our obvious differences, we must acknowledge Trump. In the same vein, he too must acknowledge that his election still means losing the overall popular vote by more than 2 million votes. Losing the popular vote by millions can be interpreted in many ways, but for those of us seeking inclusion and justice for all Americans, it means we have not lost our way home. There is a political loss, but we must reject the idea that his win represents a radical call to transform the America of the majority. The majority remains an America that values healthcare and shelter for those in need over tax shelters for the rich. The majority remains an America that cherishes fairness and paying your fair share.

For the NAACP, the nation's oldest and largest civil rights organization, the big story of this election is not merely Trump or the Democrats' loss of the electoral col lege, or even 2 million more votes being cast for Clinton. Instead, for us it's more about the sullen reality faced by millions of Americans who were unable to, or who unnecessarily struggled to cast their votes due to a gutted Voting Rights Act.

In the first election without the full protection of the VRA, we saw a return to an America of old, where southern states fresh off the end of Reconstruction utilized every manner available to disenfranchise the recently freed Negro.

In our America, voting is the cornerstone to true democracy. Without it, democracy can never be real to the masses of people seeking to transform this nation of potential into the nation its ideals say it can be. Without the vote, true democracy remains a mere reflection of truth, like Plato's allegory of the cave. In our America, truth is real and access to the vote is the sole yardstick of America's greatness as a nation. For America to reach its pinnacle, elections can never simply be about winning regardless of the cost to our ideals. It must be about moving the nation forward. Nor too can it be about gerrymandering, voter suppression, or dog-whistle politics.

Throughout this election season, the NAACP has confronted all manner of ugly, unconstitutional voter suppression, including voter purging, intimidation, and misinformation.

In the last five days of the campaign, after many months in planning, we formally launched our Selma Initiative to protect the right to vote. We targeted 6,022 precincts in seventeen states, dispatching both lawyers and laypeople alike to safeguard access to the ballot box.

On Election Day, volunteers at our national command center and on the ground across the country stood by the side of voters as they faced countless obstacles to the polls, from missing registrations to absent election judges to hours-long lines.

This is a fight we've never run from, and one we've fought in the streets, in the halls of power, and in the courts for more than 107 years.

No fewer than nine times in the past nine months, the NAACP has fought and prevailed in the federal courts against voter suppression. In Texas, our state conference saved 608,470 votes with a victorious decision from the U.S. Court of Appeals for the Fifth Circuit. In North Carolina, our state conference saved nearly 5 percent of the electorate when the U.S. Court of Appeals for the Fourth Circuit ruled that the state legislature had enacted discriminatory voting laws that intentionally targeted and disenfranchised black voters. And, right before the election, the NAACP saved nearly 4,500 voters from being purged from the North Carolina rolls.

Altogether, we mobilized our 2 million digital activists, nearly half a million card-carrying members, 2,200 local

units, and more than a hundred partner organizations both
to protect and get out the vote.

History will judge not only the courage of our volunteers but also the cowardice of those who chose repeatedly to suppress the vote rather than to make democracy
real. History may take note of the Selma Initiative, but
let us all now remember Shena Goode, a seventy-nine-
year-old NAACP volunteer who not only organized a
virtual phone bank in her apartment complex, but also
made more than 200 calls in a single day to get out the
vote. Her story is the story of the NAACP and the nation.
When civil rights are threatened, we are as persistent as
we are determined.

Now that the election is over, many of us are asking ourselves, "Where do we go from here?" For the NAACP, our
interests remain pertinent. As such, the priority for a new
Congress and a new president must be restoring the badly
broken Voting Rights Act.

During this critical period of transition, we are now
calling upon the next president to speak and act with the
moral clarity necessary to silence the mean-spirited racial
politics that have characterized recent months and left many
of our fellow citizens either snarling at one another in anger
or whimpering in fear. The more than 120 million Americans who cast ballots in this election—as well as the more
than 100 million more eligible voters who declined to vote—
deserve no less.

The NAACP stands ready to work with a new administration to realize the racial justice concerns that not only
compelled millions of people to go to the polls on Election
Day, but also inspired millions to protest in the streets in

the preceding days and months. Depending upon the new administration's fidelity to both America's ideals of liberty and the NAACP's agenda for justice, we will either be at its side or in its face. We will not let this election distract or dissuade us; the NAACP will continue to stand strong at the frontlines, advocating for voting rights, criminal justice reform, and equality for all.

WHITE PEOPLE: WHAT IS YOUR PLAN FOR THE TRUMP PRESIDENCY?

Brittany Packnett

Brittany Packnett is the cofounder of Campaign Zero and the vice president of national community alliances for Teach for America.

On the day after the election, I reached out to my white friends. Through a series of text messages and posts, I asked them a simple question:

White people: What is your plan?

No, I am not white. I know what you may be thinking: It is therefore not my burden or my responsibility to expend my energy in this way, right? I know. But this message couldn't wait.

I was tired of being continuously assaulted by my country, yet still being expected to spring to action alone. It was very clear: White people handed us Donald Trump. White people did this. And maybe (*hopefully*) not my friends— but certainly their cousins, their uncles, and their friends. As I've publicly expressed this truth, the predictably problematic refrain of "not all white people . . ." returned again and again.

Of course not all white people voted for Donald Trump.

But of the white people who voted, six out of ten did. And chances are, nine out of ten white people know them. And at the end of the day, ten out of ten white people benefit from white supremacy.

So my question to my white friends was not a call to wage war on white people. It was me interrogating whether they were ready to join or increase their effort in the war against white *supremacy*, a system that benefits few and destroys many. Understand: White supremacy is as much about mindless habits of white privilege as it is about active beliefs. It is about impact, not simply intent.

My question was really an assertion: Never should the majority of the burden to end oppression fall on the oppressed. White people must be primarily responsible for what white people cause. People of color have enough work to do for ourselves—to protect, free, and find joy for our people.

We got us.

Do you have y'all?

People keep telling us not to be so upset over losing an election. Besides the fact that we actually didn't lose, here's what you must understand: We're not sore losers. We are, rather, afraid of history continuing to repeat itself at our expense.

Of course, not everyone who voted for Trump is actively racist, sexist, or xenophobic. Most people who voted for him were not active Klan members or neo-Nazis, though, lest we forget, the Klan did find their candidate in Donald.

Listening to many Trump voters, you'll hear that they simply wanted change. My friend, the brilliant writer Clint Smith, described one such encounter—a woman who said she wanted someone who would "shake things up." When pressed about Trump's dangerous rhetoric, her response? "Sometimes he just doesn't think before he speaks."

A vote for Trump may merely have been a vote for change.

But your change is our catastrophe. And your ability to ignore the catastrophe is evidence of blinding privilege.

If he doesn't think before he speaks, will he think before he acts? Before he institutes national stop-and-frisk or guts the Affordable Care Act? Before he casts out hard-working people because of their religion or nation of origin? Before he nominates judges who take away my control of my body or before his vice president advocates for conversion therapy?

One needn't be an active white supremacist to be a danger to us. For years to come, the future will look different for people of color than it does for white people. Ignoring or deprioritizing that basic fact is more dangerous to me than a white hood could ever be.

Chances are, if you're reading this you didn't even vote for him. You may even be finally realizing that what marginalized people have been saying for years is true, because now you're in the same boat—or you're at least wading in the same dangerous tide we've been swimming against for generations.

But know this: whether you actively engage in the violent culture of hate or merely step out of the way to give it permission to persist and room to grow, you are complicit.

And white people, you give permission to this culture every day you do nothing more than have "conversations on race." You don't get to just have conversations anymore. You don't get to just wear a safety pin and call yourself an ally. You don't get to just talk while the rest of us fear for our lives because discrimination, rape culture, and xenophobia just won the White House.

Too often oppressed people are told to exhibit an inordinate amount of grace and patience while white people are "on their journey." And it's true: No one is born woke. We all have work to do and we should respect where people are. But as Dr. King reminds us, too often "*wait* means *never*," and your journey may cost someone their citizenship, their religious freedom, or their life.

My grace extends to where your responsibility begins. And it is your responsibility to know, see, and urgently help dismantle a supremacy that creates winners and losers through complicated, shrouded rules built on a basic desire to preserve power.

Let's be clear: White supremacy harms all of us. It strips humanity from both its victims and its beneficiaries. You don't need to intend to perpetuate white supremacy for its impact to be felt. It shows up in the implicit bias of the officer, the teacher, and the shopkeeper. It shows up in the health outcomes for the hood and the educational gaps for the nation. It shows up as hate when children should be too young to feel it, and fear when we're old enough to know better.

White supremacy is beneath us. It cannot persist if we seek equity and liberation.

And because it benefits you, white people, you have the primary power to crumble it.

So I ask again: What is your plan?

Hopefully, by now you've been sufficiently convinced to make one. But perhaps you need some places to start.

LEARN TO OBSERVE SUPREMACY.

You've been excusing Uncle Jim's racist jokes because he's old and from another era. You've been avoiding wondering whether your boss invited you instead of the more qualified woman of color because you make him more comfortable. You've stopped using the phrase "white supremacist" because your editors prefer the more passive, permissive "alt-right" that doesn't anger white readers.

You haven't done these things out of malice—because you may not even see them as acts of white-dominant culture.

Thus, before you confront supremacy, you must first learn to see it. You know it when someone paints a swastika. But can you see it when it shows up quietly and pervasively throughout the culture? Observing quiet, subversive supremacy is hard when it's been both natural and convenient for you during the span of your lifetime. Learn about microaggressions—and spend a day counting the ones you see. (For extra credit, ask a friend of color to do the same. Chances are you won't come up with the same number.) Unpack your invisible privilege knapsack, develop your understanding of your racial identity, and read what it means to wake up white.

Already done this? Great!

But that's just step one.

LEARN TO CONFRONT SUPREMACY. BECOME AN ACCOMPLICE— NOT MERELY AN ALLY.

In "No More 'Allies,'" Mia McKenzie reminds us of the danger of taking one comfortable step and awarding ourselves the title of *ally*, then turning right back around and being dangerous. Many of our so-called allies espoused complex, seemingly revolutionary democratic rhetoric on social media all day. But if you chose to opt out of reducing harm and protecting my real life in the name of your abstract political philosophy, you are not my ally. When the "apocalyptic productivity" you advocated or allowed comes, the productivity will protect you while the apocalypse destroys me. You are not creating a safe space for me or other marginalized people.

Keep your safety pin.

The work of freedom is messy, dangerous, and intentionally uncomfortable. Here's a simple test: if the action step you're taking isn't really costing you your comfort, chances are you're not doing enough.

I can walk past you and see your safety pin, but will you stop, film, and intervene if you see me being pulled over or assaulted? I can listen to your progressive chatter at the water cooler, but are you protecting Planned Parenthood and a woman's right to choose? You can tell me my life matters on Twitter, but will you show me my life matters when I need you to wait a day to ask me for data because the election re-sults have made me physically ill? Or that my queer cowork-ers' lives matter when their colleagues misgender them? Or that my undocumented students' lives matter when they need real protection?

Getting in the way to protect the vulnerable, building something new that empowers the marginalized, and en-dangering yourself to shield others are the acts of an accom-plice. We need no more allies—we need accomplices.

BECOME A RESOURCE, NOT AN OVERSEER.

Many of my friends wrote to me that providing funds, talent, or support to people of color and our organizations would be their immediate next steps. This is an important step that many can take and many organizations will be thankful for, but only if it remains respectful.

I cannot tell you how many offers I've received for help that come with a list of commands for exactly how we should do our work. White people who ensure people of color have access to capital from which we have historically been cut off can be helpful—but if your offer of support comes with a need to set my agenda, that's not support; that's control. And that's you giving me more of what we're fighting against.

STILL NEED IDEAS?

The question I asked my white friends resulted in several dozen responses on and offline. My friend David Rosenberg

came up with a starter plan that includes staring down hatred—and vowing to never become desensitized. My friend
Justin Cohen has upped his urgency by organizing white
educators to confront supremacy and offers a helpful (and
funny) guide to handling supremacy at the dinner table.
One friend plans to become readmitted to the bar to help
fight inevitable deportation cases pro bono, while another
pledged to talk to those in his own intersectional community: "I'm going to challenge my white LGBTQ friends more,
regardless of who they voted for. We took this for granted,
and I'm responsible." Even if it's just on Twitter, take a look
at more responses from folks just like you, making decisions
about where to start doing white folks' work.

Nothing I have suggested here is comfortable. That's
because freedom work isn't comfortable. It requires a daily
struggle of difficult choices and exhausting actions. But
every moment we choose comfort over the truth, freedom
work loses ground. We've lost enough ground; we can't afford any more. Act or don't act. Both are a choice, and both
have consequences. For the sake of the republic, my people,
and our collective humanity, I hope you choose to share
your plan and get to work.

3

IMMIGRATION

WE ARE ALL EMIGRANTS

Ilhan Omar

Ilhan Omar is the director of Policy and Initia-
tives of the Women Organizing Women Network
and a member of the Minnesota House of Rep-
resentatives. She is the first Somali American
legislator in U.S. history.

At the Democratic National Convention in 1936, the renominated President Franklin D. Roosevelt began his acceptance speech: "Here, and in every community throughout the land, we are met at a time of great moment to the future of the Nation." Today, we find ourselves at a similar moment; we must choose whether we strive for equity through the avenues of democracy or wake in bigotry's shadow. Our divisions have created a ravine in the soul of American democracy: the axiom of choice relies on humanity's better angels—our notion of self-preservation remains the only obstacle to equity.

It is essential we recognize the inherent obligation of humanity: to build community. Surviving life in a refugee camp at a young age, I find this obligation to be very real; hope and unity were essential to a fervent community. Having experienced grave injustice to the extent that we had to flee our homes, we got through each day by existing in solidarity—looking out for one another—and with the hope of one day finding a better life for our family and loved ones. My grandfather would hope aloud for what was to come, the possibilities of a free existence. His stories left me enamored of the mere concept of democratic participation— he cultivated my passion and engendered my American Dream: a life dedicated to public service and the betterment of those without.

A determined girl, I decided early on that barriers were meant to be surpassed, and that heroism is nothing more than acting with determination and compassion. We fled literal hunger and fell into the arms of a new starvation, starvation that was not merely physical: the overwhelming lack of community and compassion. The profusion of ignorance that we have seen in the results of the recent election demonstrates the hunger that currently pervades every corner of our nation. The only way to sate this hunger is to educate; knowledge is the sustenance that we must provide to all those who preach hatred, profess bigotry, and champion anti-intellectualism. Ignorance is antithetical to the nation we continue building together; we must root it out—our words and our deeds must embody love of neighbor, compassion for all, and respect and understanding.

In our nation, prejudice is institutional and rampant, leaving a majority of us doubled over under the yoke of oppression. It is easy to remain lost in post-election shock; we forget that democracy is messy and that its elegance is not aesthetic but ideological. Each of us is seeking comfort in this turbulent time, and the narrative of a Somali American Muslim woman elected at the same time as Donald Trump is easy to spin as a victory. Honestly, this makes me chuckle: never have I believed that the mere election of someone who looks like me would be an end-all to our problems. I have always known that taking the oath of office is merely the beginning.

When I first came to the United States, I knew two phrases in English: "Hello" and "Shut up." But the difficult part of going to school each day was not linguistic; it was the attitude teachers took toward our diaspora. Somalis are caricatured as the remnants of a failed state lost to terrorism and piracy, inept and in need, yet we have thrived in this land of opportunity. It is our home. I remember one day the teacher had a math problem on the board. As usual I raised my hand, knowing the answer, but the teacher didn't acknowledge me—even when no other student had their hand raised—so I got out of my seat, walked to the board, solved the problem, and quietly sat back down again. That classroom did not provide opportunity to me, so I decided to take it myself. Such ethnic biases pervade every system in our society; we must remove them. This sentiment is shared by every once-immigrant community in our nation. It is almost a rite of passage: if you can stand up to the oppression, your people can succeed.

It is not the failings of oligarchic leadership that are the cause of our suffering, but the underlying tepidity of individual efforts. To ensure progress and change, we must, with intelligence, commit to that community-building obligation rooted deeply in the human psyche. The way to prevent individual apathy is to bring everyone to the table, to build a coalition of all. It is complacent to assume that America—The Great Experiment—or any nation will inevitably provide equality. An Athenian lawmaker, Solon, is quoted as saying, "Wrongdoing can only be avoided if those who are not wronged feel the same indignation at it as those who are." That was 2,500 years ago, yet today we still decide: What does America stand for? Are we perpetrators of a false democracy in which the strong—the rich, the white—survive, and the weak—the poor, the oppressed, the disaffected— suffer in the perennial battle for justice? Or do we believe in the principle that all people are created equal? America is the never-finished attempt at cosmopolitanism—we are all emigrants.

To characterize overt xenophobia as "nativism" is not only laughable but dangerous. When we refuse to acknowledge the failings of our forebears, we not only perpetuate ignorance, but we also strengthen inherent oppression, thus cementing the same systems at which we continue to chip away centuries later. Visualizing next steps should not lead to violent revolution. We live in a free and democratic society. Change will never be top down, it must come from the roots and be nurtured, embodied by every American and manifested in our everyday actions and attitudes.

Combatting hate and reshaping our society by crafting an inclusive democracy is a great task, and we should consider ourselves blessed to be in positions of influence where we can make such a difference. It is simple: talk to people, visit with them, broaden coalitions of love and acceptance.

The precedent we set will become "storied past," so our decisions should be based on long-term strategy. As we are undoing centuries of systemic inequity, here and in every community throughout the land, we are met at a time of great moment to the future of the Nation.

UNDOCUMENTED AND #HERETOSTAY

Cristina Jiménez

Cristina Jiménez is the executive director and cofounder of United We Dream.

For all intents and purposes, Donald Trump ran his campaign against my family, friends, and community. I grew up undocumented in New York City. My parents, brother, and I moved here when I was thirteen, seeking a better life than we had in our native Ecuador, where there weren't any jobs and we couldn't afford food or rent.

Moving to Queens was a shock for my family. Learning English was a challenge. So was dealing with the stop-and-frisk racial profiling policy and the constant fear that my parents would be victims of an immigration raid. It was tough navigating a school where violence was commonplace and where a counselor told me I had no hope of attending college because of my immigration status.

But we survived and made a home. A small number of other young immigrants and I started speaking out. In those days, we used fake names because it was too dangerous to reveal our identities. But in spite of the fear, we organized, asserted our right to not be pushed around, and told the world that we were #HereToStay.

In the history books, our story looks no different from that of the Irish, Germans, or Italians before us. But in the twisted view of Donald Trump and his ardent supporters, we are a menace that needs to be wiped off the face of the country.

I'm now the executive director of a national organization of undocumented immigrant youth called United We Dream. For nearly ten years, we've helped undocumented young people recognize their own collective power. Together with our network of local affiliates and allies, we've won the ability to get driver's licenses and to pay fair tuition rates. We've protected nearly 800,000 young people across the country from deportation and allowed them to work through the Deferred Action for Childhood Arrivals Program (DACA). And from the start, we've done it while being true to our values of inclusion.

Under the Trump administration, my parents and brother could be deported. It's no exaggeration to say that tens of millions of people are terrified. Our members have reported a sickening increase in bullying and harassment, both in schools and on the street.

Immigrants, Muslims, women, queer people, artists,

and so many others have worked for years to come out of the shadows in order to live in the light as their true selves; the Trump movement is determined to send us back to a life of terrified silence in the dark.

We will not be terrorized. We will not be silenced.

Indeed, if Trump gets his way, our very existence may become an act of civil disobedience. I am asking all people of conscience to join us at this critical moment and resist.

What has grounded me in this time of deep fear is the resilience of our communities and the eagerness of non-immigrants to fight alongside us for a country that is just and inclusive of everyone. This is the only way forward: local, intersectional organization across movements to protect our communities from hate, racism, and exploitation.

But fighting for justice in this way does not mean diluting the struggles we face with a set of broad messages and strategies. It means showing up for each other when we come under attack, and showing up for each other when we have an opportunity to advance the cause of justice.

We know that this works because we have seen it work.

In Houston, Texas, a racist sheriff lost his reelection campaign in November after immigrant youth joined with black and LGBTQ allies to stop a dangerous policy that let local police work as federal immigration agents. In the county with the most deportations of anywhere in the United States, a wide range of communities worked together to shine a light on the horrific status quo of racial profiling and incarceration in Houston. Because of cross-movement organizing, injustice became a front-page issue, and in that context, those defending the racist status quo lost.

United We Dream members are undocumented, we are U.S. residents and citizens, we are black, white, Muslim, AAPI, and LGBTQ people. We represent the full spectrum of the American experience and are more determined than ever to fight for the right to live as our full authentic selves and to remain unafraid to be loud, bold, and visible in our journey to build a more equitable world.

This is the way forward: local grassroots organizing, the daily practice of using an intersectional and cross-movement lens, and the discipline to do the hard work of building together with diverse communities who share values and vision. We must strategize together because our futures are intertwined. *Black, white, Muslim, immigrant, LGBTQ, AAPI communities—all* people must build a multiracial movement of love to confront the hateful headwinds we are expecting in the years to come.

Now is the time for white people, people of color, and people of conscience to link arms with Muslims and undocumented people to build a protective network of love between these communities and Trump's deportation force.

It is time for all of us to consider our place in history, because we are entering a historically significant time.

Life in 2017 will not be the same as it has been this year. There are men who are determined to put women, black people, Latinos, immigrants, workers, Muslims, and queer people "back in their place." They view political activists with disdain and will stop at nothing to reassert control over all levers of power. But we have come too far, and we won't turn around.

Most people voted against Donald Trump, and the

movements for black lives and for immigrant rights have revealed truths about the way our government works—truths that cannot be unseen. We are #HereToStay and ready to march. Fueled by a burning passion for justice, we are the ones we've been waiting for.

4

WOMEN'S RIGHTS

WELCOME TO THE RESISTANCE!

Gloria Steinem

*Gloria Steinem is a political and social activ-
ist and organizer, and is widely recognized as
one of the leaders of the second-wave feminist
movement.*

Once upon a time, there was a schoolyard bully who had a
very rich father. This kid pretended he earned all his money
on his own, gave huge parties, and, like so many guys with a
superiority complex, was obsessed with controlling women,
as well as black, Mexican, Muslim, and other classmates he
thought were lower on the totem pole.

Soon, he discovered that if he told a lie that was big
enough, simple enough, and he kept repeating it enough, a
lot of people would believe him.

So, when this bully decided to run for student body president against the smartest and best-liked girl in the school,
he called her a liar. He said she cheated and should be ex-

pelled. Though she was more honest and hardworking than the other students, the bully kept planting seeds of doubt.

Finally, some students decided they didn't trust the bully *or* the smart girl—after all, girls are not supposed to be smarter than boys—so they didn't vote at all. Some voted for the bully because they hated school, and the smart girl was always trying to make school better. Also, the bully's friends thought he could make them rich, too, even without school. And so, because some classes with just a few students counted as much as those with a lot of students, the bully won. His followers took over the school. True, some pretty different students had won in the past—though all were male and only one wasn't a white guy. But this was the first-ever bully.

In reality, this seems to be where we are. We have a president-elect who was endorsed by the Ku Klux Klan, who believes global warming is a fiction invented by the Chinese to harm American business, who demonizes people by religion and geographic region, who thinks girls and women are only for sex and work with no power over their own lives. Though the primary reason people gave for voting for Trump was his business success, he actually kept going bankrupt in order to pass his debts on to others. If he had just invested the money he inherited he would have been way richer.

As his lawyer, biographer, and first wife all have testified, he does believe in the Big Lie. For instance, though Hillary Clinton was judged by independent fact-checkers to be more honest and accurate than *any* of her 2016 opponents, Trump dubbed her "Crooked Hillary," and threatened to prosecute and imprison her. It worked. After months of this in the media, she went from fourteen years of being chosen by Americans as the most admired woman in the world to having the same mistrust rating as a disgraced Richard Nixon.

I don't want to be too scary here, but there was another leader whose party was elected by people who were having hard times and who wanted their country to be great again. His name was Adolf Hitler. He, too, promised to make his country great again, campaigned against racial and religious minorities, championed Aryan working men, ridiculed a women's movement that was more politically powerful in Germany than in any country in the world, surrounded himself with beautiful and subservient white women, and captivated crowds with slogans chanted in beer halls—the Twittersphere of his day. He also padlocked family planning clinics, declared abortion a crime against the state, and made a political alliance with the church, even though he was no more religious or monogamous than Trump.

Fortunately, this country has a much longer tradition of democracy, diversity, and human rights than did Germany. Most important of all, we have a strong and free press to counteract the Big Lies—especially the fake facts and hundreds of phony news sites that helped to elect Trump. For instance, on Facebook and Instagram, African Americans, white liberals, and young women, all likely Hillary voters, were targeted in final pre-election weeks with a $150 million campaign that presented one 1996 comment of Hillary's about gang members as if she were talking about all African Americans. On Election Day, 95 percent of black female voters and 85 percent of black male voters cast their ballots for Hillary, yet the turnout was lower than expected. How many more would have voted if they hadn't felt wrongly accused?

So what are you and I going to do?

First, we must remember that we who didn't want Trump as president are the majority. Hillary Clinton won the popular vote by more than 2.5 million; a margin bigger than those that put Kennedy or Nixon in the White House. Given ongoing recounts, Trump may have lost by more votes than any popularly elected president in U.S. history. In addition, every major issue he has opposed has majority support in public opinion polls, from reproductive freedom to the reality of global warming. Though some Trump voters are living in an impossible dream—38 percent wish the South had won the Civil War—most are suffering economically and were just voting for anyone outside of Washington. Trump has appointed more billionaires to his cabinet than any president-elect in history; it's unlikely that those who have profited from inequality will work to decrease it. That justifiable anger that swept Trump and his crew *in* can sweep them *out*. After all, Trump can transplant his hair and cover his gelatinous body with designer suits, but he can't have a character transplant. He will remain the bully he has always been—self-obsessed, thin-skinned, short on facts, long on grandiosity, and very predictable.

Second, when we elect a possible president, we tend to think our job is done and we can go home. Now that we've elected an impossible president, we will look up less and look to each other more. We will see that electing one African American president and nominating one female president was only a beginning. Any chief of state only holds a finger to the wind. We must become the wind.

At times like this, Gandhi used to say, "The truth is revealing itself." I think that's happening now. No more fictional phrases like "post-racist" and "post-feminist." No more waiting to be told what we *should* do, giving up our own wisdom and authority. We will do whatever we *can*.

For instance:

- Because Trump came up through mainstream corporate media that depend on ratings and ads, not through any political party, the media must now take some responsibility and refuse to give the next un-fact-checked despot the estimated $2 billion in free exposure that was given to Trump. Also, we who write and publish anywhere, on the web or in print, must ourselves value verifiable facts, not only the number of "hits" a headline attracts. If this election has taught us anything, it's the deep value of facts and the danger of the Big Lie.

- Because Trump didn't strengthen the current Republican Party, which is controlled by extremists—beginning with the racist Democrats who left their own Party after it supported the Civil Rights Act of 1964—there is a chance that centrist Republicans can take their party back. Older Republican women remember when this party was the first to support the Equal Rights Amendment. Right now, they could take their feminist daughters and granddaughters to local caucuses where delegates to the National Republican Convention are elected. In four years, there might be a bloody struggle, but in eight years, there could be a centrist Republican Party again.

- Because women still make up 85 percent of all purchases at point of sale, we could make good use of the Boycott Trump app—available at www.Keep AmericaGreat.us—that lists products and services benefiting Trump's interests. We can boycott them and e-mail a company itself to explain why: for instance, because it advertised on *Celebrity Apprentice*, the "reality show" that presented Trump as if he were an admirable and successful businessman. We have dollar power and vote power. We can use both.

- Because paying income tax is also voting with dollars, and Trump and Vice President–elect Pence are threatening to cut off government funds to Planned Parenthood, each of us could object by deducting a sum from our personal income tax and sending it directly to Planned Parenthood instead. In the past, some Americans refused to pay the portion of federal income tax that went to the war in Vietnam. Of course, the IRS collected it eventually, but the process had huge nuisance value; an alternate way of voting. In this case, Planned Parenthood would benefit right away.

These possibilities are in addition to the street demonstrations, online exposés, marches in Washington, D.C., and support for, say, Standing Rock, the largest protest in a century by Native Americans. Right now, thousands of Water Protectors are blocking the Dakota Access Pipeline, which is endangering the environment—and in which Trump is an investor. After all, our Constitution doesn't begin with "I, the president." It begins with "We, the people."

The next few years are uncharted territory, but there is one deep and present parallel. We have learned that family violence is the paradigm of all violence—other than that used in direct self-defense—and in family violence, the most dangerous time is the moment just before or just after escape. A woman, or anyone escaping, is most likely to be beaten or killed then because she or he is escaping control.

I think this country is in a time of danger because most of us are escaping the control of a few of us. We are about to become a nation with a majority of people of color. This will make us more connected to the rest of the world. Yet there is still a white minority that fears that they will be treated as they have treated others.

Just as we would never tell a woman, man, or child to stay in a violent household, so we will never go back to the old hierarchy. Despite ongoing threats, at home and in other countries—including a very racialized and gendered terrorism—we are now the majority. And we have many leaders who inspire democracy, who model it, and who know that we are linked, not ranked. Yes, this is a time of maximum danger, and we must act together, and look after each other.

But maybe, just maybe, we are about to be free.

NOW IS THE TIME TO DOUBLE DOWN ON WOMEN'S LEADERSHIP

Ilyse Hogue

Ilyse Hogue is the president of the National Abortion Rights Action League (NARAL) Pro-Choice America.

After the election results came in, I kept thinking: it's not surprising that the first woman within grasp of the White House failed to get there. It wasn't even surprising that the very qualities that made Hillary Clinton such a credible candidate—her vast experience, comprehensive grasp of policy, and willingness to think first and speak second—were the very things that were weaponized against her in the campaign.

That's how it often goes with women. We are all too familiar with the feeling of being held to a different set of standards—like how you can lose an election while receiving more votes than anyone else. At this point, it appears Hillary Clinton won the popular vote by more than 2 million votes—receiving more votes for president than anyone who has ever run for the office, other than Barack Obama.

So the fact America got not the first woman president, but instead a man who ran on sexism, racism, and xenophobia, should probably feel familiar; and maybe it does in the devastation that has gripped so many since the election.

But we cannot let the losses of the last year limit our vision for the country we love. To do so would be to learn the wrong lessons from our long march toward equality, and to risk teaching a new generation of Americans that when the arc of justice doesn't bend in our direction, we retreat. Now is the time to regroup, to understand the lessons from our loss, and to find the path forward so that we can march again with pride and purpose.

The history of social movements shows that the path to justice and equality is always marked by setbacks. Civil rights heroes endured unspeakable abuses and backlash against their victories. LGBT Americans were denied basic rights and often forced into the shadows. While these setbacks can sometimes feel more like a free fall down a dark hole, experience teaches us to take heart. Our path forward is illuminated all around us. It is in the spirit of the large majority of Americans who share our fundamental values of freedom, justice, and opportunity for all. To harness our collective strength, we need simply to come together to organize, organize, organize—and demonstrate the leadership that our nation deserves.

Our journey forward has to start with recommitting to our core values as progressives. We know that race, gender, geography, education, and age all affect our economic prospects, and that ensuring dignity and a fair shake for all means engaging in authentic conversations to find real community-based solutions. The fight against Wall Street greed and the fight to create economic opportunity for families are not at odds. Nor is the struggle to protect women's rights at odds with the fight to ensure everyone has access to quality health care. The values that unite our communities are not in conflict; they're intertwined. Recognizing these intersections is critical to help us build momentum right now for the difficult work ahead.

This is doubly true for women. Since women historically have known more barriers to opportunity than men—and women of color face the seemingly endless web of racism and sexism—we must understand how identity has affected opportunities to organize effectively. This will help us avoid balkanizing a movement that needs to operate in unity.

It is important to remember that Donald Trump is not the first or only politician to use misogyny to advance a divisive partisan agenda. From Texas requiring women who seek abortion to bury the fetal remains, to Alabama's refusal to extend Medicaid health coverage to families living in poverty, to Indiana moving to shut down health clinics and criminalize abortion providers—the groundwork has long been laid for the misogyny coming out of Donald Trump's mouth.

These actions flow from a belief that women are lesser; that our place in the world is to be subservient and that our preferences can be ignored. This outdated view found a welcome home in Trump's presidential campaign and has already become firmly entrenched in his administration.

These are the forces we must take on in order to move

our country forward. As a movement, we have a responsibility to fight for women as they try to provide better lives for their children. We must expand economic opportunity so that all Americans can work hard to get ahead and achieve their dreams. And we must reach across racial, ethnic, and class lines to understand our common values and shared destiny.

Some of this work will be in the political sphere—such as fighting the restrictive voting laws that keep so many from the polls, and ensuring that communities are never gerrymandered out of political power. But social movements have to commit beyond politics if we are truly to organize for the long haul. Service organizations and community groups can become new nerve centers and gathering places, offering aid and sanctuary while creating new bonds that help us organize and build power.

Many will rightly feel outrage at the election results. Yet we must remember that outrage is often an exhaustible resource. We need to combat the tendency to settle into a "new normal" in which we are inured to the effects of racism and misogyny. We must continue to provide authentic alternatives to the inflexible ideologies we will be fed every day.

Finally, we have to recommit to lifting women into leadership positions, and, in so doing, to reclaim our own power. And we must do so publicly and proudly. One of the telling incidents from this election was how some supporters of Hillary Clinton retreated to safe spaces to share their passion for our candidate. There were private online groups like Bitches for Hillary and Pantsuit Nation that flourished—their ranks swelling into the millions. But there were few bumper stickers and yards signs and fewer still public displays of enthusiasm for our candidate and agenda. Many women feared being bullied for showing their allegiance. And that very real threat kept us from expressing our collective power to the world.

Women in leadership create better results for everyone and more effective governing systems. Jay Newton-Small's book, *Broad Influence*, traces the data to show that when women are represented in leadership, more things get done. Decades of evidence also shows that when women have access to family planning, not only do our lives improve, but the beneficial effects extend to our families and communities, and can even increase our country's GDP.

Now is the time to double down on women's leadership, not back off. As we confront the threats that could undo decades of work toward equality, we have to gin up our courage, damn the bullies and blowhards, and demand that leadership celebrate women and girls.

Of course, we can't expect to defeat misogyny at the ballot box if we don't first stand together to confront it in our daily lives. Here we can draw inspiration from all over the world. Over the last year, across Europe, women walked out of work to protest the wage gap that robs them and punishes families. On Black Monday, last October, more than 1 million women took to the streets of Poland to protest a proposed nationwide ban on abortion, forcing the government to reverse course. And all across India in the last several years, women have come together to protest a culture of rape that has brutalized them for centuries. All of these women chose to stand up to bullies to make their voices heard—and our task is no different.

To be sure, men share a responsibility, too. As equal

members in our community, men must speak out against threats to our shared welfare, to check their own biases, and to respect women's space to be our own empowered selves. This is an all-hands-on-deck moment and we cannot afford to cede any ground.

Every successful movement for social change has come to learn that there is power in numbers. With a strong majority already on our side, we must continue to grow as we wage our battles online, in the halls of power, and in the streets.

Effective advocacy and organizing has always made the difference in movements for change. From the suffragists who won women the right to vote in 1920, to the feminism of the 1960s and '70s that won us independence over our own bodies and the right to choose our own destinies, to the reproductive justice movements of the last decade that shined a light on continuing inequities for poor women and women of color, there's no substitute for the power of working hand in hand to change minds and hearts. As a movement, we have always sparked change by bringing our collective voices into the cultural and political spheres. Today, our task is no different.

While we confront a difficult electoral loss, we cannot forget one basic fact: the majority of our country, men and women, are with us in this struggle. Our vast community is the source of our greatest strength. If we organize and mobilize we can harness that power and together create the path forward.

5

CIVIL LIBERTIES

WE WILL DEFEND THE CONSTITUTION AGAINST PRESIDENT TRUMP

Anthony D. Romero

Anthony D. Romero is the executive director of the American Civil Liberties Union (ACLU).

The proposed policies of Donald Trump's presidential campaign, if carried out once he's in office, will trigger a constitutional crisis. By the ACLU's reckoning, the Trump administration would violate the First, Fourth, Fifth, and Eighth amendments of the United States Constitution if it tries to implement his most controversial plans.

On immigration policy, for example, there is simply no way the Trump administration can deport more than 11 million people within two years of taking office. To achieve such a feat, Trump's deportation machine would have to arrest 15,000 people a day on immigration charges, seven days a week, 365 days a year.

The only way to accomplish this would be to shred the Fourth Amendment's protections against unreasonable searches and seizures. To carry out such an order, immigration agents would have to engage in suspicionless interrogations and arrests, unjustified traffic stops, warrantless searches of workplaces and homes, and door-to-door raids in immigrant neighborhoods. There can be little doubt that agents would have to rely on racial profiling and target people of Latino and Hispanic descent disproportionately, violating their right to equal protection under the law regardless of their race or national origin.

After rounding up undocumented immigrants "in a very humane way, a very nice way"—that would inevitably include U.S. citizens and lawful permanent residents by mistake—the Trump administration would run face first into the due process protections afforded every person inside the United States under the Fifth Amendment. It is inconceivable that 11 million undocumented immigrants could go before a judge in any reasonable amount of time. The immigration system is already seriously backlogged and under-resourced, with immigrants facing removal already waiting 635 days for an immigration hearing.

If Trump keeps them locked up, as he has proposed, he'll deprive these people of their liberty—possibly for years—without due process of law. The Southwest border region under Trump's proposals would become a police state.

In the realm of counterterrorism policy, Trump wants to do many unconstitutional things that he himself has said are "frankly unthinkable," including casting a dark shadow of suspicionless surveillance over Muslim communities and their houses of worship, simply because of their faith. By doing so, the Trump administration would infringe upon American Muslims' First Amendment right to exercise their religion freely without fear or intimidation, as well as trespass against the establishment clause, which forbids the government from singling out certain religions for disfavored treatment.

This was already attempted by the New York Police Department, with disastrous results. The NYPD's Muslim surveillance program struck fear into the hearts of Muslim New Yorkers and made them less trustful of the police. Afraid of informants and undercover cops, mosque attendance declined. People watched what they said and mistrusted each other; some even went so far as to change their dress and trim their beards to look less Muslim. In its settlement of an ACLU lawsuit against the program, the city explicitly recognized that law enforcement can do its job without resorting to discriminatory practices. Trump wants to resurrect this unconstitutional program and take it national.

And President-elect Trump's unconstitutional campaign promises didn't stop there.

In a misguided strategy to prevent foreign attacks on the United States, Trump promised to temporarily ban Muslims from entering the country and to reintroduce torture. But once again the Bill of Rights constrains him. While the president does in fact have a lot of authority in immigration matters, the government can't violate the First Amendment by unfairly singling out an entire group of people, based on their religion, for collective punishment.

Then there's torture, the tool of tyrants. Although the George W. Bush–era torture program has been widely discredited as barbaric and ineffective—not to mention illegal—Trump has been unequivocal in promising that he will bring back waterboarding and "a hell of a lot worse than waterboarding." Waterboarding, along with the rest of the Bush administration's "enhanced interrogation techniques," violates international law as well as the Eighth Amendment, which prohibits the government from inflicting cruel and unusual punishments. The same goes for methods he would approve that go "beyond waterboarding."

As a candidate, President-elect Trump also promised to "open up our libel laws" so that when the media writes things he doesn't like, "we can sue them and win lots of money." This is preposterous. There are no federal libel laws to "open up." Legal claims for libel arise under state laws, over which a President Trump would have no control. But his campaign promise is nothing to laugh about, because it shows his contempt for First Amendment values and the free press.

For ninety-six years, the ACLU has neither opposed nor supported any candidate for office. We did not endorse either Hillary Clinton or Donald Trump. But in the face of Trump's stated agenda, our job will be to muster all the legal arguments we can to derail and deter the president-elect's patently anti–civil-liberties proposals.

The Constitution and the system of government it created will survive the Trump presidency. Our institutions—particularly our courts—are stronger than the will of one man. But we are preparing for the fight of our lives, because the very freedoms guaranteed by the Constitution appear likely to face a sustained attack by the president of the United States.

When that day comes, make no mistake: we'll be seeing him in court.

HOW TO COMBAT DONALD TRUMP'S DANGEROUS THREATS TO A FREE PRESS

Trevor Timm

Trevor Timm is the cofounder and executive director of the Freedom of the Press Foundation.

At no time in modern history has a presidential candidate been as hostile to press freedom and the rights of journalists as Donald Trump.

In the eighteen months leading up to his election, Trump threatened to sue newspapers or journalists over a dozen times, while vowing to "open up libel laws" to make it easier to take newspapers to court. He attacked and insulted members of the media almost daily and blacklisted countless news outlets over the course of his campaign. He blamed "freedom of the press" for a terrorist attack in New York, said the press has "too much protection" under the First Amendment, and much more.

At the same time that the press finds itself under un-precedented threat, journalists' jobs have never been more important. It's not an exaggeration to say that the Fourth Estate will be Trump's only check on power in his first term in office. His own party holds both the House and the Senate, and he will soon control appointments to the branch and the divided Supreme Court as well.

Leaks and whistleblowing have never been more noble and more urgent. Adversarial journalism will be paramount to holding the Trump administration accountable, and it will have to be done in the most hostile atmosphere possible.

So what do we do? Well, there's no doubt it's going to be an uphill and sometimes dangerous battle, but on at least one front journalists do have tools they haven't had in the past: new technology that can enable whistleblowing even in the era of mass surveillance.

But first, there is some relatively good news in all of Trump's scary proclamations: he seems to have a fundamental misunderstanding about how free speech works. In reality, there is no federal libel law for him to "open up" it's the First Amendment itself that prevents him from actually winning any lawsuit he's filed against the press in the past. Half a century of settled Supreme Court precedent—led by the landmark case *New York Times v. Sullivan* in 1960—gives journalists in the United States broad protections against being sued for libel for reporting on information public figures don't like.

It's a different threat, however, one that was rarely mentioned on the campaign trail, that is much more of an imminent danger to journalists and the public's right to know: Trump's ability to spy on journalists, prosecute their sources, and stifle stories in the public interest will be immense—and sadly, we have the Obama administration partly to thank for this.

Before Trump came along, the Obama administration, by most accounts, had the worst record on press freedom since Richard Nixon. Despite coming into office promising the "most transparent administration ever," the Obama administration fought *for* government secrecy at almost every turn. His Justice Department expanded the use of spying powers on journalists' e-mails and phone calls; gutted reporter's privilege, which is the principle that reporters can protect their sources from being forced to testify against them in court; and prosecuted more sources and whistleblowers than all other administrations combined.

Instead of reining in the NSA and the U.S. government's massive intelligence and surveillance apparatus, Obama entrenched and expanded some of those powers—powers now in the hands of a man once accused of spying on his hotel employees at his Florida resort and cataloging the sexual liaisons of his powerful hotel guests. Once during the campaign, in response to a question about hacking his political enemies, Trump even declared: "I wish I had that power, man, that would be power."

Sadly, there is little the law can do to stop him from using the FBI and Justice Department from increasing surveillance on the phone calls and e-mails of journalists (or dissidents or critics for that matter). There remains no federal shield law that would provide a very high bar anytime the government wants to subpoena a journalist to testify or spy on them—in part because when Obama came into office, he opposed a strong shield bill. The only thing protecting journalists now are internal Justice Department guidelines that Trump can rip up on his first day in office if he so chooses.

Given it will be very difficult to rely on laws to protect their rights, reporters, activists, and whistleblowers will be forced to rely on technology and encryption to protect them where government checks and balances cannot. And *this* is where journalists now have an advantage.

Thanks to advances in encryption technology since the Snowden revelations in 2013, it is now easier than ever to use end-to-end encrypted communications to speak with sources so that the government can never secretly go to Google or AT&T or any other third party provider and demand messages. When your communications are end-to-end encrypted, it means even those third parties don't have access to the content.

Suddenly, it seems, many people are acutely aware of how vulnerable they are to government spying. Signal, the open source gold standard for encrypted messaging—which everyone should download whether or not you're a journalist—has seen a 400 percent increase in users since the election of Trump. Other more popular messaging applications already encrypt conversations end-to-end by default too, without any user intervention. Facebook's WhatsApp and Apple's iMessage will encrypt any communications users have with someone also using that app, and collectively allow more than a billion people to send and receive messages that only the sender and receiver can read.

Sadly, Signal, iMessage, and WhatsApp are anomalies compared with standard practices. Tech companies like Google work off a business model that encourages them to keep services such as Gmail *not* end-to-end encrypted, so they can scan all our communications to serve us appropriate advertisements.

This is a critical miscalculation. Tech companies should be encrypting everything possible in the lead up to the Trump presidency, because once he takes office it may be too late. More importantly, ordinary citizens should be demanding this of them. There's no law that prevents it, and the technology readily exists to allow them to provide it.

Robust digital security for journalists, however, requires training and persistence. More will be needed than messaging apps to fully protect reporters and sources from being spied on by the Trump administration. Encryption isn't going to protect everything you do.

After all, much of government spying these days is done through the collection of metadata—that is, not the content of your communications, but who you call, when you call them, for how long, and from where. This type of information can paint an intimate picture of your life without ever touching the content of your texts or calls. (Think about it: if you call an abortion clinic, or a suicide hotline, or Alcoholics Anonymous, anyone spying on you could have a pretty good idea about what you're doing without listening in.)

This is another area where tech companies need to step up to the plate, or users should talk with their feet and leave services that don't. Tech companies like Google and Facebook store a wealth of metadata on all their users for long periods of time, even though there's no law saying they have to. Tech companies should be figuring out exactly what data they absolutely need to operate and stop storing literally everything else.

In addition, there's the increased risk of hacking, the

tool Trump yearned for on the campaign trail. If the government can hack your computer—something the FBI has wanted to expand the rules on for years—all the encryption in the world isn't going to save you. While it ultimately may be impossible to stop a determined attacker, there are simple steps all users can take to make it harder on hackers of all stripes. Simple and somewhat boring measures like using a password manager to create unique and complicated passwords for every site you use and turning on two-factor authentication for your e-mail and social media accounts can go a long way to protect you.

We have to remember, though, that encryption and digital security are only tools for helping journalists hold those in power to account. There's no doubt the press finds itself between a rock and a hard place post-election: confidence in the American media has dropped to record lows, and the president-elect uses his bully pulpit to insult and demean them regularly. There's only one answer: adversarial investigative journalism at its toughest and most unsparing.

It would be wise to remember the last time in our modern history when a presidential campaign was threatening journalists with libel suits, insulting reporters at campaign events, blacklisting media outlets based on his mood, and yearning to spy on journalists at will. The president who led that campaign, Richard Nixon, went down in history as the first who was forced to resign. Why? Because of journalists who did their job in the face of enormous pressure.

6

CLIMATE CHANGE

DONALD TRUMP IS BETTING AGAINST ALL ODDS ON CLIMATE CHANGE

Bill McKibben

*Bill McKibben is the Schumann Distinguished
Scholar in environmental studies at Middlebury
College and the founder of the global climate
group 350.org.*

President-elect Donald Trump has already begun to back off
of some of his promises: Maybe not all of Obamacare has to
go. Maybe parts of his wall will actually be a fence. Maybe it's
okay to have some lobbyists running the government after all.

But I fear he won't shrink from the actions he has promised on climate change: withdrawing the United States from
the Paris Accord, ending President Obama's Clean Power
Plan, and okaying every new fossil-fuel plan from the Key-
stone XL pipeline on down. He won't back down because

those are hard-to-hedge choices and because he's surrounded by climate-change deniers and fossil-fuel insiders
who will try to ensure that he keeps his word.

So let's be entirely clear about what those actions would
represent: the biggest, most against-the-odds, and most irrevocable bet any president has ever made about anything.

It's the biggest because of the stakes. This year has been
the hottest year recorded in modern history, smashing the
record set in 2015, which smashed the record set in 2014. The
extra heat has begun to steadily raise sea levels, to the point
where some coastal U.S. cities already flood at high tide even
in calm weather. Global sea ice levels are at record lows, and
the oceans are 30 percent more acidic. And that's just so far.
Virtually every scientific forecast says that without swift action in the next few years to cut carbon emissions, this crisis
will grow to be catastrophic, with implications for everything from agriculture to national security that dwarf our
other problems.

It's the most against-the-odds bet because at this point
there's so little scientific dispute about climate change. Researchers have spent three decades narrowing the error
bars and establishing an ever-clearer picture of the future.
There's always the chance that scientists have overlooked
something, but it's by now so narrow a chance it hardly deserves that description.

And it's the most irrevocable bet because the next few
years are crucial. This makes global warming unique: If you
take away Obamacare, poor people will suffer until something replaces it—which would be bad, but that suffering
would not make it harder to fix the problem later. Climate
change, however, comes with a time limit, which is why se-

nior scientists last week were saying that if Trump carries through with his wager, it might well be "game over." If he loses his bet, he will have cost us the last years in which we might have made a real difference.

Against all this, Trump has merely the conviction that climate change is a hoax. It's a conviction more or less shared by the man he has put in charge of his energy and environmental transition team, Myron Ebell of the Competitive Enterprise Institute, and a handful of other climate-change deniers at websites such as WattsUpWithThat.com. Some, like Ebell, are funded by the fossil-fuel industry, and others are quite sincere freelancers who have involved theories about how some of the thermometers measuring the planet's climate have been placed too near to airport runways or believe that sunspots or cosmic rays or "natural cycles" will soon cool the Earth. They are contemptuous of the consensus science (the product of "a lot of third-, fourth- and fifth-rate" researchers, says Ebell) and of anyone who takes it seriously. (Pope Francis, in his encyclical on climate change, was "scientifically ill informed, economically illiterate, intellectually incoherent and morally obtuse," says Ebell.)

It's easy to see why these kinds of pronouncements might appeal to Trump. It's not just that they're spoken in the brash language he likes to use, but they made it easy for him to justify, say, his promises to restore the nation's coal mines to their glory days. It would indeed be much easier for all concerned if global warming were hogwash.

But as far as anyone knows, he has never tested his beliefs by sitting down with scientists for even a cursory examination of the data. So someone who has his ear needs to tell him that the opinions on which he's relying are marginal at best.

And that friend might remind him, too, of the difference between issues governed by opinion and those governed by fact. If you don't think poor people should get subsidized medical care, that's ugly, but it's an opinion you're entitled to hold. Science isn't like that: the heat-trapping properties of the carbon dioxide molecule simply are. Which is why, even if we fail in our efforts to stop Trump from making his bet, it's important for history to note what's going on. One man is preparing to bet the future of the planet in a long-shot wager against physics.

PROTECTING OUR PLANET

Michael Brune

Michael Brune is the executive director of the Sierra Club.

Donald Trump will assume office as the only head of state in the entire world who rejects the scientific consensus that mankind is driving climate change. And despite vague promises to keep "an open mind" on climate change and the important international agreements to combat it, we already know that the Trump administration will be a boon to fossil-fuel polluters that want to avoid commonsense safeguards while receiving carte blanche to mine and drill on our public lands.

So does that mean the United States can no longer make progress on climate action and clean energy? Absolutely not. Despite living in his own fact-challenged reality, not even Donald Trump can change the fact that the world is heating up, and that we are reaching a tipping point. He can't change the fact that clean energy sources are outcompeting dirty fuels like coal, gas, and nuclear power all over the country. He can't change the fact that both the market and the climate movement are aligned to replace coal plants with clean energy—nearly 250 plants to date, with many more to come. He can't alter the fact that both public opinion and the marketplace strongly favor clean energy over dirty fossil fuels. Scientists, students, business leaders, and activists are moving this nation beyond dirty fuels to clean energy, and Donald Trump can't reverse that tide.

Making progress in the face of a hostile administration is not just wishful thinking; we have a historic precedent. The Sierra Club's grassroots Beyond Coal campaign got its start during the administration of George W. Bush, and it successfully defeated most of the new coal plants proposed during that administration—184, to be exact. We can win the same kinds of victories under the Trump administration, but only if we refuse to flinch from the struggle for climate action, land and wildlife protection, and environmental justice.

First, though, let's acknowledge that although we made significant environmental progress under President Obama, our nation's challenges run much deeper than any one issue or any one president. Even if Trump were somehow forced from office, that would not by itself solve the racism, misogyny, and xenophobia that existed before his rise. It wouldn't eliminate the hatred in our public discourse and in our communities. It wouldn't magically create a 100 percent clean energy economy, nor would it alleviate the economic pressures that millions of families face in their daily lives. The election of Donald Trump is a result of those underlying issues, and they must be addressed.

One way we can do that is by ensuring that the transition from a dirty fuels economy to a clean energy economy is, above all, an equitable process. Too many Americans, especially in the Rust Belt, have been left behind by the rush to create a global economy. So-called free trade agreements like NAFTA and the proposed TPP have hollowed out many communities. Residents of those communities are rightfully demanding an economy that works for them, and we in the environmental community owe it to those citizens to show how a future based on clean energy will make their lives better. We have to make sure that the opportunities of that renewable energy economy are shared widely.

Just as important, though, is that we continue to stand in outspoken solidarity with all those who were targeted by Trump during the presidential campaign. People of color, Muslims, immigrants, women, the disabled—millions of Americans were singled out and attacked by Donald Trump before he even took office. People sometimes ask me why the Sierra Club can't just "stick to protecting the environment." Trump's election shows exactly why. If we turn a blind eye to inequality, racism, misogyny, and xenophobia, then we will be forced to deal with the consequences, and those consequence affect everything, including environmental progress.

Meanwhile, we can expect efforts to roll back the Clean Air and Clean Water Acts—basic safeguards that have protected Americans for decades—as well as attempts to drill or mine for oil, gas, and coal in the most ecologically sensitive places on the continent.

The Sierra Club already has several immediate strategies for fighting back, and we've already begun implementing them.

Our legal program is shining a light on corruption to prevent sweetheart deals between the next administration and big polluters. Our public lands team is planning how to defend the historic public lands protections achieved during the Obama administration and earlier. That defensive work will play out in the courts, in Congress, in statehouses, in the marketplace, and in the streets.

At the same time, we are intensifying our focus on growing the clean energy economy at the state and local levels, helping to grow the blossoming number of cities (twenty as of this writing) that have committed to 100 percent clean energy. We've already been winning important victories in state houses, on public utility commissions, on ballot initiatives, and in corporate boardrooms—and we will keep winning.

We refuse, however, to be in a defensive crouch for years to come. We will be relentless in our fight nationally and internationally against fossil fuels and for clean energy and smart transportation policies at the city and state levels.

To that end we will also aggressively recruit new activists, volunteers, and donors to our cause. The Sierra Club's grassroots activists are the foundation of our strength, and we will work to engage and activate a new generation of Sierra Club activists and climate movement leaders. If you are ready to join that fight, we welcome you. You can make an incredible difference by becoming part of this movement.

Although it might seem like everything changed on Election Day, it didn't. Our values have not changed. We still believe in justice, fairness, and equality. We believe in democracy. We believe that it's a good idea to replace fossil fuels with clean, renewable energy. We believe people have a right to drink clean water and breathe clean air. We believe it's vital to care for our public lands, protect wildlife and our last wild places, and encourage people to get into the great outdoors.

Those basic values are shared by millions upon millions of Americans. What's more, despite the ultimate outcome of the election, the fact remains that a clear majority of voters rejected Donald Trump's ignorance, misogyny, and racism. Those same millions will stand up every day to ensure that he can't roll back the progress we've made in recent years.

7

RELIGIOUS FREEDOM

THE ULTIMATE WAKE-UP CALL

Linda Sarsour

*Linda Sarsour is the executive director of the
Arab American Association of New York and
the cofounder of the first Muslim online organizing platform, MPowerChange.org.*

I am a Palestinian-Arab-Muslim-American, daughter of immigrants, a political activist, and a woman—basically, you
don't want to be me in 2016. I am not going to lie to you—I
was as devastated as many of you were with these election
results. But I have no regrets. I did everything I could to
ensure that a man as incompetent as Donald Trump would
never set foot in to the oval office. But here we are and here
he is, the president of the United States of America.

During this election, we heard proposals to register Muslims and spy on Muslim centers and mosques. It
seemed outlandish and unconstitutional, and it sent many
of our fellow Americans into a state of rage. For the past

fifteen years, policies such as these have already had a deep impact on Muslim communities across the United States, and our fellow Americans were mostly silent. In 2003, under the Bush administration, the Department of Homeland Security implemented a program called the National Security Entry-Exit Registration System (NSEERS) that required males over the age of sixteen who were not U.S. citizens or legal permanent residents and who were nationals of any of twenty-four Muslim-majority countries to register with the federal government. About 110,000 Muslim men complied with this program; 10 percent of them were placed into deportation proceedings.

This program sent shockwaves through the community. Many families decided to self-deport, and traveled back to their home countries in fear of what may happen to Muslims who registered. Entire neighborhoods were affected, like the Coney Island Avenue area in Brooklyn, New York, home to the largest Pakistani community in the world outside of Pakistan. I remember serving as a volunteer translator at 26 Federal Plaza in New York City for some who registered. I will never forget the faces of these men, many from my own community—faces full of fear and uncertainty.

Spying on mosques, on community centers? We already know what that feels like. In 2011, the Associated Press released a blockbuster investigative report that revealed through leaked documents that the New York Police Department engaged in unwarranted and baseless spying on New York's Muslims—in mosques, cafés, grocery stores, Islamic centers, schools, and the Muslim Student Association. My organization—a social service and advocacy organization in Brooklyn, New York, that works with refugees, asylees, and immigrants—was found to be a direct target of the New York Police Department's surveillance programs. Imagine being part of a community that is already seen as suspect—targeted by systemic racial and religious profiling, even under a more progressive administration. We believe these activities will only be amplified under a Trump presidency. Our concerns are valid; they have already been our daily reality.

I know for many of us the election results are confusing. The question everyone is pondering is "What do we do now?" You are hearing different pieces of advice, some of which are conflicting, on what we do now under a Trump administration, on how we respond to key cabinet appointments of open white supremacists/nationalists, anti-Semites, anti-immigrant, and anti-women zealots, and Islamophobes . . .

I want you to keep telling yourself: "THIS IS NOT NORMAL. THIS IS NOT NORMAL. THIS IS NOT NORMAL." Repeat until it sinks to the deepest of your core. The minute you decide this is normal, this is just how it is, the minute you decide that appointing a white supremacist to one of the highest, most influential positions in the White House (and a long list of them follows, and I don't mean Trump)—that is the minute that you give up. Stay vigilant. Stay focused. Stay OUTRAGED. Perpetual outrage is what's going to fuel our movements right now. In the face of this crisis, the time is now to follow your heart. You know what feels right. Think. Contemplate. Don't just follow blindly. Stay informed, read articles, verify sources, diversify your news intake. Knowledge is power. Ignoring what's happening is not going to help you or anyone else.

One of the most important things we can all do as Americans is to begin investing in relationship building. Do you know your neighbors? Do you know who leads the local community-based organizations in your neighborhood? Do you know the heads of the local churches, local mosques, and temples? Do you know who your local elected representatives are? If no, start now. If yes, how can you deepen those relationships so that they are transformative and not simply transactional?

As you build these connections, do not choose alliances based on fear—choose alliances based on shared principles and values and radical love for our shared people. Be cautious of those who delay or never condemn the enemy of white supremacy. When you are listening to advice at work, in school, at a conference, at a lecture, online, or in the media—ask yourself if the person speaking is credible? Does their advice make sense based on who they are? For example, would you take advice from a dentist on your foot problem? This is the time for all of us to stay in our lanes. We must respect the talents and experiences of one another, and leverage our respective knowledge for the greater good.

The immediate work we need to do is to protect the most marginalized communities and those who have been directly attacked by Trump and his appointees. We must focus on making our local communities sanctuaries for undocumented immigrants and Muslims. We must raise our voices now, as a preventative measure, against the reinstitution of a Muslim registry program. And if it does happen—we must call on people of all religions and backgrounds to find the moral courage to register as Muslims. Donald Trump did not win the popular vote. We need to remind him every

single day that we will not sit back idly in the face of injustice against any of our fellow Americans. We can agree
to respect the presidency, but we do not have to respect the
president. I will not respect a president that campaigned by
vilifying and dehumanizing Muslims, Mexicans, Syrian refugees, black people, and women.

One of the most memorable moments for me during this
election was when I went to give a lecture at a public university. It was a packed crowd of young people, mostly people
of color, and I talked about what social justice looks like in
2016. At the end of my lecture a student from the Muslim
Student Association stood up to ask a question. He asked,
"Who were the people who lived in the United States at the
time of Japanese Internment camps?" He continued with
such passion, "Who were those Americans who allowed for
their Japanese American neighbors and their children to be
picked up and taken to camps on this U.S. soil, who were
those people?" I had no answer for him at the time. He took
my breath away. A few days later while sitting in my office
in Brooklyn, his voice came back to me, and I sat and re-
flected. I finally had the answer. Those people were the silent
majority.

I hope this election is our ultimate wake-up call—a
wake-up call for the silent majority who have been silent in
the face of so much injustice in recent years. Silence is violence. We cannot and will not be the generation that allows
our country to live again the darkest moments of our history. We must remember that our work over the next four
years is not just for us, but also for the generations to come
who are counting on us.

As for me, I am staying unapologetically Muslim. Not

only is that my choice, but I also have every right in these United States to be unapologetically Muslim. I am committed to keeping my voice loud, my feet in the streets, and my mind focused on real justice and equality for all. I am not afraid, because fear is a choice—I will choose courage. The future of this nation is in our hands. The question is: What are we willing to sacrifice? What history will we write together? I believe in us. We got this.

POST-ELECTION SERMON

Rabbi Sharon Kleinbaum

Rabbi Sharon Kleinbaum is the spiritual leader of Congregation Beit Simchat Torah, in New York City, the world's largest LGBT synagogue. She has served as a commissioner on New York City's Commission on Human Rights, and on the U.S. State Department's Religion and Foreign Policy Working Group's Sub-Working Group on Social Justice.

This sermon was delivered on November 11, 2016.

Last week at this time we observed Kristallnacht—November 9, 1938. The night when five years of Nazi propaganda and rhetoric erupted into physical violence. Now here we are, just one week later, wondering if we are on the brink again.

Clearly, this is a moment of crisis for all of us. We won't actually know what this historical moment is until we are able to look back. But I have talked to enough congregants to understand some of the things you're feeling: Confusion. Shock. Grief. Despair. Anger. Sadness. Frustration. Fury. Panic. Terror. Grief. Grief. Grief. But also: Determi-nation. Resilience. Hope. Optimism. Might. Solidarity. Community. Courage.

My first job is to tell you that your grief is real. That the trauma is real, and you need to be kind to yourself about it. If somebody yells at you, "How come you're not moving more quickly?" Say, "You know I need to lie here and sob a few more days." That's okay.

It is okay to experience deep grief and it is okay to understand that at some point you'll emerge and be able to act. Both things can be true. There is no way to force your way through grief. You do have to let the feelings happen. But there are some things that are helpful. Don't isolate yourself. Isolation doesn't help, even though you may feel that you want to be alone right now. You may need somebody to say, "You know what? I'll take over for a couple of days. You cry; here's my shoulder. Then I'll cry on yours."

Don't try to medicate your grief away. You actually have to feel it. But also be kind to yourself. Imagine the things that give you strength when you are feeling good and force yourself to do them.

There will be moments when it will feel like a roller coaster; that's what it has been like for me this week. There are moments when some realization comes upon me suddenly and I'm aware of yet another level of grief.

And yet there are times, on that roller coaster, when I'm not in free fall. When I can actually feel the track below me—if I can extend the metaphor. There were a bunch of victories on Election Day, including a number of glass ceilings that were shattered. Ilhan Omar, a Muslim Somali woman, elected to the House of Representatives! And we have four new women senators. Four new wom-en senators! Catherine Cortez Masto, the first Latina senator! We've had other victories as well. GLSEN—the Gay, Lesbian, and Straight Education Network—put out a map of what the electoral college vote would look like if it had just been eighteen-to-thirty-four-year-olds voting; Hillary Clinton would have gotten 504 electoral votes, definitively winning the presidency. That makes us hopeful for the future.

As it is, Hillary Clinton won the popular vote of this country. That means that our vision for the United States, which so many of us feel was betrayed, is shared by the majority of Americans who voted.

And yet huge numbers of Americans did not turn out to vote. What are we going to do about that? We have to see it as our responsibility to encourage and strengthen the institutions of this country.

And then there's the Electoral College. We started to do something about it when Al Gore lost the electoral vote, and then we got distracted. Can we do something about it this time?

Yes, even as we're working through the grief, we have to act.

Our first priority is to protect the most vulnerable among us. We all know the story of Noah, of the flood overtaking the world. Well, right now there is a flood overtaking the world. And we have to build an ark and invite onto it those most at risk.

How do we build this ark, so that there is room for us all to survive this flood and come out strengthened? That's going to be our challenge. What are the institutions that have to be fortified? What are the relationships that have to be deepened? What are the changes that have to take place in our personal lives and in the lives of our communities? How do we ensure that this terrible setback does not destroy us?

What are we here at Congregation Beit Simchat Torah going to do, in addition to helping to protect the most vulnerable members of society? The first thing we're going to do is educate ourselves.

I want to really understand fascism. I want to understand the history; I want to understand the politics. And guess what—we happen to have members of our community who know this stuff. We're going to start bringing in people and programs to better educate ourselves about what fascism looks like and how it has been resisted, successfully, at other moments in history. We don't have to reinvent the wheel. We've been at the precipice before.

Second, we're going to make sure that our prayers and our religious lives give us strength. We need to sing. We need to pray. We need to be joyous. We need to celebrate Shabbat. We need to bake rainbow challahs down in the kitchen together. We need to make sure that we continue building a full and meaningful and joyous life. That is an important form of resistance.

We are going to continue thinking of ways that we can interrupt the narrative of hatred.

Third, we have to figure out what kinds of political activism make sense for us to engage in. Just because we don't have the answers right now does not mean the answers don't exist. But it *does* mean we have to engage with the political process and think about ways that we can be effective politically. It's not just about making noise. Though I love making noise. I love being a street activist. But we also have to think about what works politically. We're going to do it as a community here at CBST and we're going to do it in all the other communities we're part of.

The fourth thing we're going to do is make connections. Today, our clergy visited a mosque to express solidarity. We're going to continue to reach out to our Muslim brothers and sisters and say, "We are together." We don't need anybody's permission to do that. We don't need a big political infrastructure to do what we did today: show up at a mosque with a little sign that says, "WE JEWS SUPPORT OUR MUSLIM NEIGHBORS."

And yet to show that support, we may have to do more than just hold signs. The president-elect has said he intends to register every Muslim in this country. Well, let him try. Because if he tries to register Muslims, there are going to be a lot more Muslims to register than he ever imagined. Millions of us Muslims!

We as Jews love to say, "Never again." We love to say, "Where were the gentiles in Europe and in the United States when we were being rounded up for the concentration camps?" We love to point the finger and say that no one hid my family. We love to say that no one stood up when our families were ripped out of homes and forced onto trains— not necessarily by German Nazis but by Ukrainians, by

Lithuanians, by Poles who had been our neighbors. Well, here is our chance, people! Muslims are now being threatened. And we are saying to Muslims, "We are going to stand with your community. If you have to register, we're going to register with you."

We love to say, "Never again." Well, never again means never again. Never again means never again!

We are put on this planet with a purpose. We are now alive in a moment of history that will show us what that purpose is. Have hope. Do not fear. Okay, fear—but do not let fear paralyze you. Let God help give you the strength to do the things you know are right.

We are put on this planet with a purpose. Now we're blessed to find out what that purpose is.

HOW OUR FEAR CAN BE TURNED INTO A POWERFUL MOVEMENT

M. Dove Kent

M. Dove Kent is the executive director of Jews for Racial & Economic Justice.

The November 2016 election has pushed many of us past the brink of what we thought possible in American politics. In its wake, we are left with an ongoing and daily fear for the safety of our communities and the futures we envisioned for ourselves.

I offer that it's okay to be afraid.

We have been told that when we are afraid, we are weak. While this can be true, it is also too simple. As individuals and communities, we all have weaknesses and vulnerabilities, and in order to build strength we must identify them, with clarity, and let them teach us.

This means fear can be a tool. Fear can lay bare what is at

stake; it can push us to dig deeper with each other and create new openings for action. Under these conditions, we can let our fear bring us toward honest and thoughtful assessment about where we need to change course. Together we can ask: What does our fear tell us about how to build a powerful movement that will create safety and wellbeing for all of our communities?

In these challenging times, we need to give thought to the broader strategies we're using to bring people together to organize. To contribute to that conversation, here are ten lessons to keep our communities safe and build the power we need to ensure that all people can thrive. They are drawn from the successes and failures, both experienced and in-herited, from twenty-five years of community organizing at Jews for Racial & Economic Justice (JFREJ), alongside our many brave partners.

I. GET BACK TO GOOD OLD GRASSROOTS ORGANIZING.

We learned from this election that there are no shortcuts. Voting is just one aspect of what it means to live in a de-mocracy. We need to participate in democracy in between elections by building powerful social movements that hold our elected officials accountable and put the needs of our communities front and center. Fighting to win real change means growing movements person by person and commu-nity by community. We have to build power by building a robust base of members; developing and supporting lead-ers; forming and supporting coalitions; and waging strategic campaigns to win real change. Social media campaigns and flashy communications strategies will get us new listeners, but will not ultimately win us our rights. And grassroots organizing doesn't just change laws; it changes people. Ai-jen Poo, director of the National Domestic Worker Alliance, teaches that when we build a powerful base of people to lead transformative campaigns, those people are transformed through being part of something larger than themselves. This transformation is what makes it possible to keep building enough power to last beyond any one election or issue campaign.

2. CONNECT THE DOTS.

We need to shift much of our energy from the national stage to the local. This means focusing neighborhood-by-neighborhood on the needs of our people. But working locally doesn't mean organizing in isolation from each other—quite the opposite. We've got to look across the globe for insight, solidarity, and models for successful change. There is a critical need to build a twenty-first-century *grassroots internationalist* vision. This means building mutual solidarity, forged over time, between the frontline communities most directly impacted by poverty and racial injustice here in the United States and around the world. Grassroots Global Justice Alliance is a great example of a coalition making these empowering connections real: creating alliances between those who are suffering from the intersecting impacts of economic injustice and white supremacy, and creating opportunities for change in their towns and cities.

3. INVEST IN PARTNERSHIP.

The people who will bear the brunt of this administration's policies must be the ones to chart the way forward. For our resistance to be effective we will have to coordinate between communities to create the trusting relationships that will carry us through the rough seas ahead—not just for the next four years, but for the next forty. This means that white communities and white-led institutions will have to build or strengthen relationships with the grassroots organizations and leaders already working in black, Muslim, Arab and South Asian, Latino, immigrant, and other communities targeted by the administration. White leaders will have to practice trusting and following the leadership of partners in those communities most directly targeted, and committing even more deeply to that partnership when things get tough.

4. GET OUTSIDE AND GET OVER OURSELVES.

We need to work effectively with new partners and new communities whom we may have limited exposure to. We need to get out of the boxes we've been in to form new alliances across neighborhoods and sectors. As racial justice and civil rights activist Linda Sarsour writes elsewhere in this book:

> One of the most important things we can all do as Americans is to begin investing in relationship building. Do you know your neighbors? Do you know who leads the local community-based organizations in your neighborhood? Do you know the heads of the local

churches, local mosques, and temples? Do you know who your local elected representatives are? If no, start now. If yes, how can you deepen those relationships so they are transformative and not transactional?

We've got to find new frameworks for common ground, and end the litmus tests that separate us. This doesn't mean we need to alter our core political convictions, but it does mean that the thinner lines in the sand that previously divided us must be erased. We will need to find a way to get over ourselves, and quickly, if we are to be of service. We need to create a movement large enough to hold people from across a political spectrum and generous enough to be welcoming to people just stepping into organizing for the first time.

5. IDENTIFY PATHS TO POWER.

Throughout the presidential campaign, longtime organizer Linda Burnham asked our organizations, "What is your path to power?" We need to create pathways to power that include all of the tools at our disposal, and all of the leaders in our communities. This means partnering across grassroots organizing and electoral organizing. It means moving money from electoral campaigns into frontline community work, while also moving people from our grassroots movements into elected positions of power. We have been too cautious in our assessment of who our future leaders are. We need to create pathways for leaders in Muslim, immigrant, poor and working-class communities, and communities of color to bring their direct experience of discrimination to bear on changing policy. Ejeris Dixon, organizer and director of Vision Change Win, asks us to support new progressive candidates in the next election to provide "obstruction, community protection and to reduce the harm of state violence." For those who have become totally disillusioned with elections, Dixon reminds us, "We do not need to believe in the electoral system to participate in electing officials for harm reduction."

6. RECOGNIZE WE ALL HAVE A ROLE TO PLAY.

We need to raise up the people in our communities who haven't been stuck in the same old conversations and stale politics; they can lead us into the bold new places that we will need to go to survive Trump's America and most effectively shield those who will be its first targets. This doesn't mean that we don't each have a role in facing the crisis before us, or that we should dismiss the wisdom of those who have been in the trenches for years. Rather, it's our responsibility to "position people who have been survivors to teach others," as Mijente Director Marisa Franco tells us. We need a "leaderful" movement, as the Movement for Black Lives frames it, with abundant roles for everyone, and flexibility and humility on all sides.

7. CHANGE HOW OUR MONEY MOVES.

We need to change foundations to put decision-making into the hands of directly impacted communities, not just those that have amassed wealth over generations. We need to push foundations to end the competitive framework of today's philanthropy that pits organizations against each other for resources. No foundation or donor should ever again ask an organization, "What do you do differently from other organizations?" thus forcing them to one-up their closest allies. We should all be asking each other: Who do you lift up? Who do you follow? Who will you emulate? Who will you support? Caitlin Breedlove teaches a practice of asking ourselves regularly: Who's win will be a win for us too? We have to move in that direction and move philanthropy with us.

8. COUNTERACT THE WAYS OPPRESSION HAS GOTTEN INSIDE US.

We have to understand the ways in which oppression—racism, misogyny, Islamophobia, anti-Semitism, homophobia, transphobia—has been internalized by all of our communities, with profound psychological and social effects. We're all walking around impacted by what our parents, grandparents, great-grandparents, and community elders went through, and we continue playing those experiences out on each other in ways that can be harmful. We have collective healing to do, changing the ways we live and organize together, if we're going to be able to forge a different kind of movement. Academic and activist Andrea Smith writes, "No one goes through five hundred years of genocide and white supremacy undamaged. Consequently, organizing work and healing cannot be separated." At JFREJ, we've been unpacking the ways in which anti-Semitism has impacted our community, how the effects of violence, displacement, and discrimination against our families over the generations has led us to carry feelings of terror and isolation below the surface. We're healing through storytelling and connection, and in this moment of rising anti-Semitism, we're giving our allies opportunities to stand up for us, creating a different story for the future.

9. HOLD COMPLEXITY: GET HONEST AND MESSY.

We have to be able to hold a complex political analysis that leaves room for a lot of grey. The results of the election may be a result of white supremacy *and* an unjust economic system. When we try to reduce situations to make the case for our own campaigns, it doesn't ultimately help the larger movement. The truth is, we can end multiple oppressions at the same time—and we'll need to. We've got to understand the interlocking systems of white supremacy and Christian hegemony; to see the ways in which racism, Islamophobia, and anti-Semitism pit our communities against each other; and to get honest and messy with each other to be able to dream bigger and broader.

10. RECOGNIZE HOW WE NEED EACH OTHER.

There's been a lot of finger pointing about who is responsible for Trump's win, and a lot of blaming of poor and working-class communities in particular. This kind of blame game against directly impacted communities isn't ever going to be a winning strategy. That's because we need a truly multiracial, multiethnic, multiclass, multigenerational social justice movement in order to win big victories. Writer and historian Aurora Levins Morales teaches that if ever we think that the real needs of our communities are at odds, then we are just not imagining a big enough vision. In the world we truly need, no one gets left behind.

We'll have to guard against the divide-and-conquer politics that let our movements break down or our communities compete against each other for what we need most. Asian American activist and development director at Caring Across Generations Jaime-Jin Lewis writes,

> All of us are sewn together by multiple identities . . . It is critical in this moment to examine where we might be a wedge unknowingly and uphold a status quo that isn't inclusive of all people. This doesn't mean we have to be silent about the challenges and struggles we face. We should identify the root causes of these challenges and work alongside others who share our struggles to undo them.

Our power depends on learning how to effectively build and accountably act as a diverse community. Ultimately, we will need profound faith: in each other, in our shared humanity, and in something greater than any of us. Faith in the face of fear carried my ancestors and many of our ancestors through unbearable conditions. Building on faith doesn't make us weak; it is part of what makes us powerful.

8

ECONOMICS

THOUGHTS FOR THE HORRIFIED

Paul Krugman

*Paul Krugman is a Nobel Prize–winning econ-
omist and columnist for* The New York Times.

So what do we do now? By "we" I mean all those left, center, and even right who saw Donald Trump as the worst man ever to run for president and assumed that a strong majority of our fellow citizens would agree.

I'm not talking about rethinking political strategy. There will be a time for that—God knows it's clear that almost everyone on the center-left, myself included, was clueless about what actually works in persuading voters. For now, however, I'm talking about personal attitude and behavior in the face of this terrible shock.

First of all, remember that elections determine who gets the power, not who offers the truth. The Trump campaign was unprecedented in its dishonesty; the fact that the lies didn't exact a political price, that they even resonated with a large bloc of voters, doesn't make them any less false. No, our inner cities aren't war zones with record crime. No, we aren't the highest-taxed nation in the world. No, climate change isn't a hoax promoted by the Chinese.

So if you're tempted to concede that the alt-right's vision of the world might have some truth to it, don't. Lies are lies, no matter how much power backs them up.

And once we're talking about intellectual honesty, everyone needs to face up to the unpleasant reality that a Trump administration will do immense damage to America and the world. Of course I could be wrong; maybe the man in office will be completely different from the man we've seen so far. But it's unlikely.

Unfortunately, we're not just talking about four bad years. Tuesday's fallout will last for decades, maybe generations.

I particularly worry about climate change. We were at a crucial point, having just reached a global agreement on emissions and having a clear policy path toward moving America to a much greater reliance on renewable energy. Now it will probably fall apart, and the damage may well be irreversible.

The political damage will extend far into the future, too. The odds are that some terrible people will become Supreme Court justices. States will feel empowered to engage in even more voter suppression than they did this year. At worst, we could see a slightly covert form of Jim Crow become the norm all across America.

And you have to wonder about civil liberties, too. The White House will soon be occupied by a man with obvious authoritarian instincts, and Congress controlled by a party that has shown no inclination to stand up against him. How bad will it get? Nobody knows.

What about the short term? My own first instinct was to say that Trumponomics would quickly provoke an immediate economic crisis, but after a few hours' reflection I decided that this was probably wrong. I'll write more about this in the coming weeks, but a best guess is that there will be no immediate comeuppance.

Trumpist policies won't help the people who voted for Donald Trump—in fact, his supporters will end up much worse off. But this story will probably unfold gradually. Political opponents of the new regime certainly shouldn't count on any near-term moment of obvious vindication.

So where does this leave us? What, as concerned and horrified citizens, should we do?

One natural response would be quietism, turning one's back on politics. It's definitely tempting to conclude that the world is going to hell, but that there's nothing you can do about it, so why not just make your own garden grow? I myself spent a large part of the Day After avoiding the news, doing personal things, basically taking a vacation in my own head.

But that is, in the end, no way for citizens of a democracy—which we still are, one hopes—to live. I'm not saying that we should all volunteer to die on the barricades; I don't think it's going to come to that, although I wish I was sure. But I don't see how you can hang on to your own self-respect unless you're willing to stand up for the truth and fundamental American values.

Will that stand eventually succeed? No guarantees. Americans, no matter how secular, tend to think of themselves as citizens of a nation with a special divine providence, one that may take wrong turns but always finds its way back, one in which justice always prevails in the end.

Yet it doesn't have to be true. Maybe the historic channels of reform—speech and writing that changes minds, political activism that eventually changes who has power—are
no longer effective. Maybe America isn't special, it's just another republic that had its day, but is in the process of de-
volving into a corrupt nation ruled by strongmen.

But I'm not ready to accept that this is inevitable—
because accepting it as inevitable would become a self-
fulfilling prophecy. The road back to what America should
be is going to be longer and harder than any of us expected,
and we might not make it. But we have to try.

THE FIRST 100 DAYS RESISTANCE AGENDA

Robert B. Reich

Robert B. Reich is an economist who served in the administrations of Presidents Gerald Ford and Jimmy Carter, and was secretary of labor under President Bill Clinton. He is Chancellor's Professor of Public Policy at the Goldman School of Public Policy at the University of California, Berkeley.

Trump's First 100 Days agenda includes repealing environmental regulations, Obamacare, and the Dodd-Frank Act, giving the rich a huge tax cut, and much worse. Here's the First 100 Days resistance agenda:

1. Get Democrats in the Congress and across the country to pledge to oppose Trump's agenda. Prolong the process of approving choices, draw

out hearings, stand up as sanctuary cities and states. Take a stand. Call your senator and your representative (phone calls are always better than writing).

Your senator's number: www.senate.gov/senators/contact/.

Your representative's number: www.house.gov/representatives/.

2. March and demonstrate—in a coordinated, well-managed way. The Women's March on Washington is already scheduled for the day after the Inauguration —and will be executed with real skill. There will be "sister" marches around the country—in Los Angeles and elsewhere. They need to be coordinated and orchestrated. And then? 1 Million Muslims? 1 Million Latinos? What would keep the momentum alive and keep the message going?

3. Boycott all Trump products, real estate, hotels, resorts, everything. And then boycott all stores (like Nordstrom) that carry merchandise from Trump family brands.

4. Letters to Editors: A national letter-writing campaign, from people all over the country, every walk of life and every level of society, from celebrities to sports heroes to grassroots Americans. In most papers, the Letters to the Editor section is the most-read part of the paper.

5. Op-Eds: A steady flow of arguments about the fallacies and dangers of Trump's First 100 Days policies and initiatives, from name-brand think-

ers and doers to ordinary folk writing for their city's or community's newspaper.

6. Social media: What about a new YouTube channel devoted to video testimonials about resisting Trump's First 100 Days Agenda? Crowd-sourced ideas, themes, and memes. Who wants to start it?

7. Website containing up-to-date daily bulletins on what actions people are planning around the country, and where, so others can join in. Techies, get organized.

8. Investigative journalism: We need investigative journalists to dig into the backgrounds of all of Trump's appointees, in the White House and the cabinet, ambassadors and judges.

9. Lawsuits: Our version of "Drill, baby, drill" is "Sue, baby, sue." Throw sand in the gears. Lawyers, get organized.

10. Coordinated fund-raising: Rather than having every public-interest group appeal on their own, have a coordinated fund-raising program to fill the coffers of the most endangered and effective opposition groups. Is there a way to do a televised fund-raiser with celebrities raising money for the Resistance?

11. Symbolic opposition: Safety pins are already appearing. What else? What more? Make the resistance visible with bumper stickers, a label pin, a branding campaign that has great language, a great logo, a great wrist band (remember the Lance Armstrong "Livestrong" yellow wrist band—it sold millions!).

12. Intellectual opposition: Take Trump on where he's weakest—with serious ideas. I'll try to do my part. You do yours, too.

13. Serious accountability: Establish performance metrics to evaluate his delivery on campaign promises. An updated website of promises made and not kept. This is one especially suited to public policy students.

14. Your idea goes here. Call a meeting of family and friends this weekend. Come up with to-dos.

The First 100 Days resistance agenda. We're not going away.

HOW TO MAKE BLUE STATES
BLUE AGAIN

John R. MacArthur

John R. MacArthur is the publisher of Harper's
Magazine.

Nearly every liberal I know is horrified by the recent election
of Donald Trump as U.S. president. I share their anguish,
but in the dismal aftermath they seem to be lunging at explanations intended mainly to make themselves feel better:
FBI director James Comey's late reconsideration of Hillary
Clinton's private server e-mails; an unexpected eruption
of racism against Barack Obama; sexism aimed at Hillary;
Facebook's mass distribution of lies like Pope Francis's false
endorsement of Trump; the blatant unfairness of the Electoral College; a fundamental American craziness exemplified
by its fanatical gun owners; Russian hackers—the list is long.

I don't disagree that these factors were possibly significant in a contest decided by so few votes. For the most part, though, liberal commentators have somehow refused to point the finger at the principal reason for Trump's shocking victory. Working-class whites, both men and women, were enraged at the Clinton couple—and to some extent Obama and the Democratic Party—about the two trade deals that cost them so many well-paying jobs over the past twenty years: NAFTA and Permanent Normal Trade Relations with China. That these two agreements hastened the departure to Mexico and China of many hundreds of thousands, if not millions, of manufacturing jobs is no longer in dispute. New scholarship by mainstream economists has reinforced the eyewitness observations by journalists who have chronicled the steady disintegration of towns and cities across America's Rust Belt, as well as in the less unionized South. From the Economic Policy Institute, to MIT's David Autor, to Yale's Peter Schott, the tally of economic dislocation caused by trade agreements is large and its political impact obvious. I covered the gradual shutdown of the Autolite spark-plug plant in Fostoria, Ohio; by 2012 the plant's production had moved almost completely to a new facility in Mexicali, Mexico, where cheap labor is plentiful and NAFTA protects Autolite's investment. Fostoria lies partly in Wood County, which in the 2012 election voted 51.3 percent for Barack Obama against Mitt Romney's 46.5 percent. This year Wood County went 50.9 percent for Trump and 42.4 percent for Clinton.

Keep in mind that the lost income and status of factory workers isn't the only cause of resentment. The collateral damage—to public schools dependent on property taxes paid by the factories, to Main Street stores and car dealerships that have fewer customers, to local civic organizations and

sports teams with less funding and volunteers, to local sup-
pliers that serviced the plants—has been immense. Multiply
Fostoria by several thousand and you've got a depth of alien-
ation that leads to Trump, who, although he calls himself
a free trader, understood that NAFTA encapsulated all the
pent-up rage responsible for getting him elected—"NAFTA
is the worst trade deal maybe ever signed anywhere," he
hammered again and again. When he taunted prospective
black voters with the slogan "What have you got to lose?"
by voting Trump, he was also speaking to unemployed and
underemployed whites. When these unhappy people were
exhorted by the Clintons to "retrain" for the "new global
economy," they took it as insulting condescension.

And what of Obama's role in this catastrophe? After de-
nouncing NAFTA during the 2008 Ohio primary in order
to wound Hillary—he claimed it had cost Ohio 50,000 jobs
and the country 1 million—he dropped the subject and then
turned free trader. Against all tactical political logic, he continued to press for adoption of the Trans-Pacific Partnership
while Bernie Sanders attacked the agreement and Hillary
cautiously disendorsed it. Did he think voters in the Rust
Belt are deaf?

Sanders's critique of NAFTA and TPP—more authentic
than Trump's—is a big reason he carried the Wisconsin and
Michigan Democratic primaries against Clinton (he might
also have won in Pennsylvania if the Democratic primary
had been open to independents). As it turned out, these
three states made the crucial difference in the Electoral College count that put Trump over the top. It's not surprising
that at the end of May 2016, polls showed Sanders leading
in a hypothetical race against Trump by roughly 10 percent-

age points in the popular vote, while the same polls showed Clinton in a dead heat with Trump.

None of this electoral math is new. In 2002, even the less-than-brilliant free trader George W. Bush recognized the political value of slapping temporary tariffs on imported steel when he needed to shore up support in steelmaking states like Ohio and West Virginia. In 2004, despite his Iraq debacle, he squeaked by John Kerry in the Electoral College and was reelected president thanks to Ohio. A renunciation of TPP by Obama at the 2016 Democratic Convention in Philadelphia, along with a full-throated recognition of Rust Belt pain, could have changed the outcome.

The question now is how the Democrats will respond, given that Clinton's assured victory (according to the pollsters) has turned to ashes. After Bush's demoralizing success in 2004—a race in which pollsters predicted on average a 2.7 percent lead for John Kerry going into the final day of the campaign—I wrote an essay entitled "Winning Blue Collars in Red States" for an anthology similar to this one. Sadly, I find myself repeating what I said back then:

> Except for his brief flirtation with non-conformity after Vietnam, the go along to get along Kerry never defied the orthodox thinking about any issue—he voted for NAFTA and PNTR as automatically as he voted for the Iraq war resolution. And yet, the Democratic nominee for president has got to blow the whistle on the "free trade" racket—that is, if the party ever wants to retake the White House. As [Ernest "Fritz"] Hollings says, "Have you ever had a pollster that ever served in public office?" Values or no values, there are votes

available for a national Democrat who dares to put the
economic security of ordinary Americans ahead of the
greed and blindness of the free trade lobby.

My teacher on so much concerning trade politics and
employment, Hollings, the former senator from South Carolina, got right to the heart of the matter: "You think we
developed a middle class on a cheap shirt? . . . Give me a
break. I can tell you right now, the labor unions and the
G.I. Bill built the middle class in America." I couldn't agree
more, but today the unions are nearly gone, especially the
industrial unions that gave a voice to working-class aspira-
tions and the muscle to pressure timid politicians. In their
place, a disaffected proletariat has arisen that finds merit in
a billionaire con man who promises the moon. From here on
let's grant new respect for common sense: if you push people
far enough, they hit back. No matter how hard liberals try to
classify the Trump vote as ugly, chauvinistic, and ignorant,
they cannot deny the damage inflicted by the "free trade"
deals pushed through Congress by a Democratic administration they voted for.

Unfortunately, it will take more than just common sense
to get through the next four years. We have the Mad Hatter
as president, a profoundly unstable hypocrite advised by the
vicious Newt Gingrich—the same Gingrich who provided
essential Republican support to Bill Clinton in his fight
to pass NAFTA in 1993. God help Alice—she's trapped in
Trumpland with the rest of us. The only way for Democrats
to get out is to begin again to take care of the people the
party once stood for.

9

LGBTQ RIGHTS

YOU ARE NOT ALONE

Rea Carey

Rea Carey is the executive director of the National LGBTQ Task Force.

Written on November 9, 2016, the morning after the election.

I, like many Americans, had a night of little to no sleep. I started today in anger, sadness, and so many other feelings, because this country has elected an extremist president and vice president, and I fear the damage they will do. We need some time to process the news with our loved ones. Time to grieve and heal ourselves. Time to know that we are not alone.

I don't want to accept that this is the America we live in, that its promise of freedom now feels fleeting. LGBTQ people, poor people, immigrants, people of color, Muslims, women, people with disabilities, so many of us . . . will need all of us to stand together and fight for justice. I know the days ahead will be difficult.

That said, when we have given ourselves the time we need, we must move deliberately and fiercely forward—to protect what we have achieved and to think bigger and bolder about the next era of progressive change, however long it may take. We have heard their plan—mass repeal of everything from food stamps for the very poor to Obamacare to marriage equality; mass deportations of immigrants; mass dehumanization of entire communities, and much more. We must do everything we can to stop the attacks we know are coming on the most vulnerable in our nation.

We will lift each other up. We will move forward together. Through our grief we will focus our resolve on a better future.

A better future for all . . . where we all experience freedom, justice, equality, and equity. Just take a few seconds and imagine a world where we are truly free, where *you* are truly free. What will that feel like?

Did any of you dare to imagine living without fear? Did you imagine walking down any street in America holding hands with your date, wife, or husband and not fearing you might be beaten, yelled at, or spat upon? Maybe you imagined a day free from constant worry that you'd hear the news about a parent, sister, brother, friend, or partner who has been picked up by immigration officials. Perhaps you imagined a paycheck that's equal to the men in your office doing the same job. Perhaps you imagined a nation where black lives really do matter. Maybe you envisioned a time when you could check into a hotel with your husband, wife, or date and you aren't asked whether you want two separate beds. Maybe you imagined the exhilaration of dancing with your friends at a club, without having the collective posttraumatic habit of checking first to see where all the exits are.

To be free is to be safe. To be safe is to be free. We have been moving closer and closer to that day, even if some days it feels further away. But we are a powerful force for good, and we will get to freedom together. For those of us who lived through the 1980s and '90s, we know that our community is at our creative and strategic best when we are under siege. Hey, we outlasted Anita Bryant. In order to reach that day, it is going to take work and we must have each other's backs—an attack on any community is an attack on us all. We are part of every community. If Muslims are attacked, we stand together. If black people are attacked, we stand together. If Jews are attacked, we stand together. If transgender people, or immigrants, or women are attacked, we stand together. We must stand together.

The work of the National LGBTQ Task Force is to doggedly pursue the day when we are all free.

I know we are all asking ourselves what we can do, what we should do. I know some of you just want to give up. Please don't. We need you.

The Task Force has been here before, feeling defeated and feeling despair, but our over forty years of work and progress gives me the inspiration and strength to march forward. To get up after being knocked down and to fight for the communities and people so close to my heart.

Many of us are searching for what we can do today. To feel connected, to take action, strategize, and help. There will be many ways in the coming days, weeks, and months, but here are a few for today:

- **BE CONNECTED TO OTHERS.** Be with each other; it is all too easy to feel isolated. Reach out today to those you know are hurting with a kind word or call. There are hundreds of vigils and gatherings being planned across the country, organized by progressive groups coming together in solidarity.
- **TAKE ACTION.** Stand with those who are standing up for what is right.
- **STRATEGIZE.** Annually more than 4,000 LGBTQ people and others from many social justice movements come together to attend our Creating Change Conference to strategize with each other on next steps for moving forward. We invite you to join us, share what you know and learn from others.
- **HELP.** There are thousands of social justice organizations that have been and will be working together for an inclusive future of justice, equity, and freedom for all. We're all going to need your support. Make a gift to an organization you love that works for justice—and we hope you consider giving to the National LGBTQ Task Force. We all need you to make a better future possible.
- Most important, let's hold each other close.

Through our pain let our love shine brightly on one another. Let's dust each other off and start our journey again ... together.

FIGHTING FORWARD

Mara Keisling

Mara Keisling is the founder and executive director of the National Center for Transgender Equality.

In November, Donald Trump was elected to be the forty-fifth president of the United States. Transgender people and those who love us are understandably gravely concerned about what his election will mean for our families, our communities, our children, and our country. After fifteen years of significant and rapid advancement, our policy agenda to make America fair for all transgender people seems less certain.

On the campaign trail, President-elect Trump was more aggressively divisive than any candidate in our lifetimes. He has denigrated immigrants, people of color, women, Muslims, disabled people, survivors of sexual assault, journalists, and those who disagree with him. He has painted himself as a defender of those struggling economically while advocating policies that would only lock them into poverty.

Since the election, as President-elect Trump has made appointments to his cabinet and other key posts, we have seen extremist after extremist nominated for positions of trust. This is on top of his selecting Governor Pence, arguably the most anti-LGBT governor in America, as his vice president. Hopes for a fair-minded administration have dimmed.

Pence has said that the Trump administration would roll back recent LGBT equality gains. Yet during the campaign, candidate Trump posed on stage with a rainbow flag, and in his victory speech on election night, he pledged to be "president for all Americans." It is now our job to make sure our new president lives up to that promise.

Living up to that would mean keeping in place the federal policy changes that have saved and advanced the lives of transgender people. It would mean being on the side of trans children as they hope to simply go to school like other kids. It would mean speaking up for us, as President Obama has done consistently in our ongoing conversation with America. And make no mistake: it would mean being anti-racist, pro-immigrant, pro-woman, pro-Muslim, pro–disability rights, and pro-worker. Trans people need all of these things in a leader. Trans people are all of the people Trump has denigrated.

There is no doubt that we are facing challenging times, and there are still many questions about what comes next. But this is how we will get through them:

- We will do everything we can to take care of each other and keep each other safe, especially those among us who are most vulnerable.
- We will continue to build up our communities and strengthen the ties we have with other marginalized communities.
- We will continue to show the nation who we are and continue working toward the day when trans people and other people are not feared or hated.

During the next four years, we will continue to build support for a more inclusive vision of society, whether this administration slows us down or not, whether this administration likes it or not. To be clear, we will continue to fight.

Over the last two decades, we have made faster progress than any movement in American history. The progress has come through supportive and unsupportive presidents alike, because we always fight. Transgender people will fight to show the people in their lives who we are; we will fight to show America who we are; we will fight to protect our children; we will fight to advance justice and against attacks on any community; and we will fight relentlessly to defend every single advance we have made. We will not stop fighting. And justice will win.

10

MEDIA

MEDIA MALPRACTICE 2016

Katrina vanden Heuvel

Katrina vanden Heuvel is the publisher of
The Nation *magazine.*

Pop quiz: What was the defining issue of the 2016 presidential campaign?

In most previous election years, the answer to that question was relatively simple to discern. In 2008 and 2012, it was the economy. In 2004, it was national security and the Iraq War. But in 2016, it was much less clear, because the most pressing issues confronting the American people were overshadowed by outrageous headlines, phony scandals, fake news, and shameful coverage of the one-man circus that is our new president. More than in any other recent election, the role of the media itself became a central, consuming issue surrounding the 2016 election.

The media malpractice began in 2015, as ratings- and profit-obsessed networks abetted Trump's rise by granting the incendiary reality TV star free, uncritical, and unfiltered access to the airwaves. For the year, the three major evening newscasts covered Trump more than twice as much as Hillary Clinton—and more than sixteen times as much as Senator Bernie Sanders. Indeed, while lavishing obscene and wide-eyed coverage on Trump, many journalists and talking heads consistently marginalized or wrote off Sanders, who espoused a similar core message of change and revolt against our political elites.

By March 2016, according to one analysis, Trump had benefited from roughly $2 billion worth of free media attention. Subsequent election coverage didn't get much better. By late October, just days before the election, the same three evening newscasts had dedicated barely half an hour to every policy issue combined since the beginning of 2016. Climate change, trade, and other important issues received no coverage at all.

It's true that other factors—such as the candidates' basic fitness for office—were more relevant leading up to Trump's election than in any other American political contest. But that does not give the media license to ignore issues of vital importance to voters across the country. It doesn't excuse the rampant false equivalence drawn between Trump and Clinton or the parties that nominated them, nor does it justify the years of substance-free coverage of the candidates themselves.

It's true that, in print media especially, some journalists, such as David Fahrenthold at *The Washington Post*, have done remarkable reporting on Trump. But despite Trump's pathological dishonesty, racial demagoguery, and brazen disdain for the First Amendment, much of the media portrayed him as a "normal" candidate for the presidency. And many of the exceptions to business as usual actually worked to Trump's advantage. Trump got away with refusing to release his tax returns, a breach of transparency that would be considered unforgivable for any other candidate. Likewise, it's not difficult to imagine how the media would have covered another presidential nominee caught on tape bragging about sexual assault followed by a parade of women coming forward to say he groped them. Yet after the initial shock of Trump's comments dissipated, the allegations against him have become—unbelievably—old news.

On the opposite end of the spectrum was Clinton and the pseudo-scandal that would not die. In October, after FBI Director James B. Comey publicly revealed the existence of new e-mails potentially relevant to the investigation of Clinton's private server, the media worked themselves into a lather. It was apparent within hours that the FBI had not discovered anything incriminating—indeed, the real scandal was Comey's improper interference with the election—but that didn't stop much of the media from amplifying Trump's calls to "lock her up" or speculating about the electoral fallout.

More frightening still, the media has continued to treat Trump as a "normal" president-elect, despite his ongoing and entirely predictable deviations from presidential norms.

There have been other times in recent memory when the suspension of skepticism and scrutiny put the nation at risk, such as when reporters became cheerleaders for the invasion of Iraq. But even with historical perspective, this media moment is particularly dangerous and fraught.

The coverage of Trump's ascendency was not a random event. It was the result of corrosive structural changes—the collapse of local daily newspapers, excessive conglomeration, the obliteration of lines between news and entertainment, the rise of right-wing "news"—that are making it harder for media to keep the public informed on the issues that demand our attention. And yet, despite these growing challenges, the media retain extraordinary power to set agendas, shape perceptions, and decide what is and is not part of the national conversation. As long as we have a corporatized system that values clicks and ratings more than serious policy debates or the people and communities affected, the problems will only worsen.

Now, Trump's presidency will demand that we think hard about the reasons for the media malpractice. The good news is that, while the damage cannot be undone, it's not too late for the media to change course. We can enact structural reforms to revive an accountability-centered media that doesn't value profits over the public interest. We should act decisively to ensure that in future elections, the American people can rely on a free and open press to fulfill their indispensable role in our democracy.

ON POLLS, THE MEDIA, AND REBUILDING THE DEMOCRATIC PARTY

Allan J. Lichtman

*Allan J. Lichtman is a distingushed professor of
history at American University. His prediction
system, the Keys to the White House, has correctly predicted the outcomes of all U.S. presidential elections since 1984.*

The pundits have been quick to blame Hillary Clinton for
her defeat in America's presidential election. Per the new
conventional wisdom, Clinton lacked inspirational qualities.
She ran a too tightly controlled and defensive campaign. She
failed to develop a coherent theme for her candidacy. She
committed a major gaffe by calling half of Donald Trump's
supporters "deplorables."

This commentary is meaningless after-the-fact rationalization that should not be taken seriously. Up until Election Day itself, these same pundits were informing the world that Hillary Clinton was poised to complete a historic victory as the first woman to be elected president of the United States. Clinton and her campaign did not suddenly change overnight. It was the same candidate and the same campaign that the commentators had previously anointed as near-certain winners.

The pundits twisted themselves into pretzels to justify why what they assured us would happen—a Clinton victory—had not happened. The Clinton blame game provided an easy substitute for hard thinking about how presidential elections work.

Using my prediction system, the Keys to the White House, I first predicted a Trump victory in a *Washington Post* interview on September 23 and then doubled down on that prediction on October 28, just before the release of the letter from FBI Director James Comey on possibly new relevant Clinton e-mails.

The Keys uncovered the fundamental problems facing Democrats in their effort to win a third consecutive term in the White House. These included grievous losses in the midterm elections of 2014, a divisive primary contest, and the lack of a major domestic policy accomplishment or foreign policy triumph in President Barack Obama's second term.

This superficial assault on the Clinton candidacy creates the illusion that the Democratic Party can rescue itself from near oblivion by finding its own Donald Trump facsimile: the man on a white horse who will lead their party to victory. After their 2016 triumph, the opposition Republicans control the White House, the U.S. Senate, and House, as well as most state governments. Once sworn in as president, Trump will break the deadlock on the Supreme Court and ensure Republican control of the judiciary for the next generation at least. In effect, the Democrats have become a shadow party in America.

The eight years of the Obama presidency may be largely erased from history. Republicans have promised to repeal or substantially modify the Affordable Care Act and weaken the regulation of business. They would reverse the progress that Obama has made in combatting climate change and repudiate his executive orders on immigration, the environment, gun control, and minimum wages. As for the Supreme Court, a reminder is in order. President John Adams served four years in office and his Federalist Party subsequently unraveled. Yet his appointee John Marshall reigned as Chief Justice for more than thirty years and put the imprint of Federalist principles firmly on the U.S. Constitution.

A rebuilding Democratic Party cannot play the pundit's blame game. The party must offer a progressive alternative to the Republicans that speaks directly to the needs of ordinary Americans, irrespective of race. Bernie Sanders provided a blueprint during the primary campaign with a focus on the transformation to a new green economy and on rectifying America's yawning disparities in wealth and income. However, the Democratic Party cannot follow Sanders down the rat hole of protectionism.

To the great detriment of his party, Senator Sanders has somehow transformed protectionism from an icon of America's right-wing icon into a "progressive" panacea. In fact, the Democrats can never beat their opponents on the issue of trade, which favored Donald Trump in this year's campaign. Sanders claimed that free trade agreements have cost the jobs of many Americans, because U.S. businesses can't compete with low-wage operations abroad. Yet there is little or no concrete proof that free trade agreements cost Americans substantial numbers of jobs. But a return to protectionism would mean much higher prices for consumer goods, with working-class Americans feeling the most pain.

Although economists rarely agree on anything, the clear majority affirm that free trade is good for the American economy. A 2006 survey of American Ph.D. economists published in *The Economist's Voice*, found that, "the overwhelming majority (87.5%) agree that the U.S. should eliminate remaining tariffs and other barriers to trade."

In truth, the future of American jobs lies not in protectionism, but in the transformation from a fossil fuel economy to the new economy of the future, based on clean, renewable sources of energy. The old smokestack and mining jobs are not coming back to America. Companies scarcely need coal miners anymore; they just blow off the tops of mountains to get at the coal.

The rebuilding of America's infrastructure offers additional prospects for job creation. Infrastructure repair was a major focus of President Obama's stimulus package, which many Republicans opposed. Somehow, Democrats have let Donald Trump seize this issue for himself, even though he remarkably proposes to spend vast sums on infrastructure while also cutting taxes, expanding the military, and reducing the deficit. However, Republican opposition to Trump's program may give Democrats an opportunity to retake the initiative on job-creating infrastructure projects.

As part of its rebuilding, the Democratic Party needs

to rededicate itself to grassroots organizing. The party supposedly had a superior organization on the ground in 2016. But the Democrats failed to deliver the kind of turnout they needed at least in part because its ground game emanated from the top down. The widespread anger and protests among its base voters in the wake of Trump's victory provides an opening for lasting bottom-up organizing.

The Democratic Party has in the past risen from the ashes. In the 1920s, the Republicans controlled the national government and nearly every state government outside the South. The tide turned after the Great Crash of 1929 began the nation's longest and deepest depression. However, the depression by itself did not revive the Democratic Party. Franklin Roosevelt's liberal New Deal reforms that gave hope and benefits to ordinary Americans and a grassroots base in the burgeoning union movement completed a realignment that led to Democrats winning all but two presidential elections from 1932 to 1964, and controlling Congress for all but four of these years. Only another New Deal will rescue the Democratic Party from near oblivion. It need not take another Great Depression to initiate a new era of progressive change.

A reconsideration of how elections really work also requires the media to move past poll-driven horserace journalism. Polls are not predictors. They are snapshots that simulate an election at a single point in time, but are abused and misused as predictors. A journalist doesn't need to get out of bed in the morning to write a story about the so-called presidential horserace, in which candidates sprint ahead or fall behind according to campaign events as the pollsters keep score.

Polls have become the driving force behind campaign

strategy, coverage, and analysis. Polls foster the impression of a race that doesn't exist because they continuously simulate elections that don't take place. The truth is that no one understands the relationship between polls and subsequent elections. As polls have become ubiquitous, the media have tilted away from covering campaign speeches and events in their own right and toward reporting how the speeches and events played in the polls—or how the polls shaped the speeches and events in the first place.

The polls also screen for so-called "likely voters," even though no pollster knows who will actually vote or has accurately reported an early vote. Thus, the so-called margins of error reported with polls (e.g., plus or minus 3.5 percent) are misleading because they represent only sampling error and presume that the poll is otherwise 100 percent accurate, including in its screen for likely voters. Actual error will be larger than sampling error and may well be systematic rather than random.

The so-called probability of victories and defeat for candidates produced by "experts" like Nate Silver are equally misleading. These probabilities look precise and scientific, indicating, for example, in Silver's final forecast, a 71.4 percent probability of a Clinton win. However, these forecasts fall victim to the fallacy of "false precision." Nate Silver and other such purveyors of win-loss probabilities do not conduct independent scientific analysis. Nate Silver is a clerk. He compiles polls; his seemingly precise probabilities are no more accurate than those underlying polls are. Silver and other compilers cannot know whether the polls are right or wrong, and if wrong, in which direction.

The pundits who relied on polls and poll compilers tied

themselves in knots to explain the results of this year's presidential election. The day before the election they were explaining why Hillary Clinton was almost certain to win and why Trump had run a campaign that disqualified him for the presidency in the eyes of most voters. A day later they had to explain why what they had said would not happen actually did happen. Their explanations amount to unprovable, after-the-fact rationalizations.

A turn away from the polls and toward the big picture of elections would suggest a new way of campaigning. Candidates should always run as though they are going to win, articulating honestly and forthrightly the policies that the candidate believes will best serve the nation. What no party should do is reprise the conventionally prescribed nostrums for winning elections—improving the technology of campaigning or running endless negative ads. Such tactics are futile because they do not influence the fundamental forces on which elections turn. In the final analysis, the parties have nothing to lose and everything to gain in terms of a mandate for governing. They should actively lead the public, and tie issues into a unifying forward-looking theme, rather than following polls.

THE BRAINDEAD MEGAPHONE

George Saunders

George Saunders is the author of numerous books of fiction, including Pastoralia *and* Tenth of December.

Imagine a party. The guests, from all walks of life, are not negligible. They've been around: they've lived, suffered, own businesses, have real areas of expertise. They're talking about things that interest them, giving and taking subtle correction. Certain submerged concerns are coming to the surface and—surprise, pleasant surprise—being confirmed and seconded and assuaged by other people who've been feeling the same way.

Then a guy walks in with a megaphone. He's not the smartest person at the party, or the most experienced, or the most articulate.

But he's got that megaphone.

Say he starts talking about how much he loves early

mornings in spring. What happens? Well, people turn to listen. It would be hard no to. It's only polite. And soon, in their small groups, the guests may find themselves talking about early spring mornings. Or, more correctly, about the validity of Megaphone Guy's ideas about early spring mornings. Some are agreeing with him, some disagreeing—but because he's so loud, their conversations will begin to react to what he's saying. As he changes topics, so do they. If he continually uses the phrase "at the end of the day," they start using it too. If he weaves into his arguments the assumption that the west side of the room is preferable to the east, a slow westward drift will begin.

These responses are predicated not on his intelligence, his unique experience of the world, his powers of contemplation, or his ability with language, but on the volume and omnipresence of his narrating voice.

His main characteristic is his *dominance*. He crowds the other voices out. His rhetoric becomes the central rhetoric because of its unavoidability.

In time, Megaphone Guy will ruin the party. The guests will stop believing in their value as guests, and come to see their main role as reactors-to-the-Guy. They'll stop doing what guests are supposed to do: keep the conversation going per their own interests and concerns. They'll become passive, stop believing in the validity of their own impressions. They may not even notice they've started speaking in his diction, that their thoughts are being limned by his. What's important to him will come to seem important to them.

We've said Megaphone Guy isn't the smartest, or most articulate, or most experienced person at the party—but what if the situation is even worse than this?

Let's say he hasn't carefully considered the things he's saying. He's basically just blurting things out, and even with the megaphone, he has to shout a little to be heard, which limits the complexity of what he can say. Because he feels he has to be entertaining, he jumps from topic to topic, favoring the conceptual-general ("We're eating more cheese cubes— and loving it!"), the anxiety- or controversy-provoking ("Wine running out due to shadowy conspiracy?"), the gossipy ("Quickie rumored in south bathroom!"), and the trivial ("Which quadrant of the party room do *you* prefer?").

We consider speech to be the result of thought (we have a thought, then select a sentence with which to express it), but thought also results from speech (as we grope, in words, toward meaning, we discover what we think). This yammering guy has, by forcibly putting his restricted language into the heads of the guests, affected the quality and coloration of the thoughts going on in there.

He has, in effect, put an intelligence-ceiling on the party.

Last night on the local news I watched a young reporter standing in front of our mall, obviously freezing his ass off. The essence of his report was, Malls Tend to Get Busier at Christmas! Then he reported the local implications of investigation: (1) This Also True at Our Mall! (2) When Our Mall More Busy, More Cars Present in Parking Lot! (3) The More Cars, the Longer It Takes Shoppers to Park! and (shockingly): (4) Yet People Still Are Shopping, Due to, It Is Christmas!

It sounded like information, basically. He signed off

crisply, nobody back at NewsCenter8 or wherever laughed at him. And across our fair city, people sat there and took it, and I believe that, generally, they weren't laughing at him either. They, like us in our house, were used to it, and consented to the idea that some informing had just occurred. Although what we had been told, we already knew, and although it had been told in banal language, revved up with that strange TV-news emphasis ("Cold WEATHer leads SOME motorISTS to drive less, CARrie!"), we took it, and, I would say, it did something to us: made us number and more accepting of slop.

Furthermore, I suspect, it subtly degraded our ability to make bold, meaningful sentences, or laugh at stupid, ill-considered ones. The next time we felt tempted to say something like, "Wow, at Christmas the malls sure do get busier due to more people shop at Christmas because at Christmas so many people go out to buy things at malls due to Christmas being a holiday on which gifts are given by some to others"—we might actually say it, this sentiment having been elevated by our having seen it all dressed-up on television, in its fancy faux-informational clothing.

And next time we hear someone saying something like, "We are pursuing this strategy because other strategies, when we had considered them, we concluded that, in terms of overall effectiveness, they were not sound strategies, which is why we enacted the one we are now embarked upon, which our enemies would like to see us fail, due to they hate freedom," we will wait to see if the anchorperson cracks up, or chokes back a sob of disgust, and if her or she does not, we'll feel a bit insane, and therefore less confident, and therefore more passive.

There is, in other words, a cost to dopey communication, even if that dopey communication is innocently intended.

And the cost of dopey communication is directly proportional to the omnipresence of the message.

The generalizing writer is like the passionate drunk, stumbling into your house mumbling: *I know I'm not being clear, exactly, but don't you kind of feel what I'm feeling?* If, generously overlooking my generalizations, your gut agrees with my gut in feeling that the nightly news may soon consist entirely of tirades by men so angry and inarticulate that all they do is sputter while punching themselves in the face, punctuated by videos of dogs blowing up after eating firecrackers, and dog-explosion experts rating the funniness of the videos—if you accept my basic premise that media is getting meaner and dumber—we might well ask, together: Who's running this mess? Who's making Sean Hannity's graphics? Who's booking the flights of that endless stream of reporters standing on the beach in the Bahamas, gravely speculating about the contents of a dead woman's stomach?

Well, that would be us. Who runs the media? Who *is* the media? The best and brightest among us—the most literate and ambitious and gifted, who go out from their homes and off to the best colleges, and from there to the best internships, and from there to offices throughout the nation, to inform us. They take the jobs they take, I suspect, without much consideration of the politics of their employer. What matters is the level of Heaven that employer occupies. The national is closer to God than the local; the large market looks down upon the small; the lately ratings-blessed floats slowly up, impressing the angels whose upward movement has fizzled out, because they work for losers.

There's no conspiracy at work, I don't think, no ill will, no leering Men Behind the Curtain: just a bunch of people from good universities, living out the dream, cringing a little at the dog-crap story even as they ensure that it goes out on time, with excellent production values.

How does such a harmful product emanate from such talented people? I'd imagine it has to do with the will to survive: each small piece of the machine doing what he or she must to avoid going home to Toledo, tail between legs, within the extant constraints of time and profitability, each deferring his or her "real" work until such time as he or she accumulates his or her nut and can head for the hills, or get a job that lets them honor their hearts. (A young friend who writes content for the news page of an online media giant e-mails me: "I just wrote this news headline for my job: 'Anna Nicole's Lost Diary: "I Hate Sex."'' If anyone wonders why Americans aren't informed with real news it's because of sell-out corporate goons like me who will do anything to never deliver a pizza again.")

An assistant to a famous conservative opinion-meister once described her boss to me, a little breathlessly and in the kind of value-neutral mode one hears in this milieu, as being one of the funniest, most intelligent, high-energy people she'd ever met. I believed her. To do what he does must take a special and terrifying skill set. Did she agree with his politics? She demurred—she did and she didn't. It was kind of beside the point. He was kicking much ass. I immediately felt a little gauche for asking about her politics, like a guy who, in the palace, asks how much the footman makes.

The first requirement of greatness is that one stay in the game; to stay in the game, one must prove viable; to prove viable, one has to be watched; to be watched, one has to be watchable; and, in the news business, a convention of Watchability has evolved—a tone, a pace, an unspoken set of acceptable topics—that bears, at best, a peripheral relation to truth. What can be said on TV is circumscribed, subtly, by past performance, editing, and social cues, and, not so subtly, by whether one is invited back.

This entity I'm trying to unify under the rubric of the Megaphone is, of course, in reality, a community tens of thousands of people strong, and like all communities, it is diverse, and resistant to easy generality, and its ways are mysterious.

But this community constitutes a kind of *de facto* ruling class, because what it says we can't avoid hearing, and what we hear changes the way we think. It has become a kind of branch of our government; when government wants to mislead, it turns to the media; when media gets hot for a certain story (i.e., senses a ratings hot spot), it influences the government. This has always been true, but more and more this relationship is becoming a closed loop, which leaves the citizen extraneous. Like any ruling class, this one looks down on those it rules. The new twist is that this ruling class rules via our eyes and ears. It fills the air, and thus our heads, with its priorities and thoughts, and its stunted diction.

This is a ruling class made of strange bedfellows: the Conservative Opinion King has more in common with the Liberal Opinion King than either does with the liberal and

conservative slaughterhouse workers toiling side by side in
Wichita; the Opinion Kings have friends in common, similar
ambitions, a common frame of reference (agents, expected
perks, a knowledge of the hierarchy of success indicators, a
mastery of insider jargon). What they share most is a desire
not to be cast down, down from the realm of the rarefied air,
back to where they came from.

There's a little slot on the side of the Megaphone, and as
long as you're allowed to keep talking into the Megaphone,
money keeps dropping out of the slot.

Seasons pass. What once would have evoked an eye roll
evokes a dull blink. New truisms, new baselines, arise. A
new foundation, labeled Our Basic Belief System, is laid, and
on this foundation appear startling new structures: a sud-
den quasi acceptance of, say, the waterboarding of prisoners,
or of the idea that a trial is a privilege we may choose to
withhold if we deem the crime severe enough.

At this point I hear a voice from the back of the room, and
it is mine: "Come on, George, hasn't our mass media always
been sensationalistic, dumb, and profit-seeking?"

Of course it has. If you want a tutorial on stupid tonal-
ity, watch an old newsreel ("These scrappy Southern Yanks
are taking a brisk walk toward some Krauts who'll soon be
whistling Dixie out of the other side of Das Traps!"). We
were plenty able to whip ourselves into murderous frenzies
even when the Megaphone was a baby, consisting of a handful of newspapers (Hi, Mr. Hearst!), and I suppose if we went
back far enough, we'd find six or seven troglodytes madly

projecting about a village of opposing troglodytes, then hogging down there, hooting pithy slogans, to eliminate it on the fallacious power of their collective flame fanning.

But I think we're in an hour of special danger, if only because our technology has become so loud, slick, and seductive, its powers of self-critique so insufficient and glacial. The era of the jackboot is over: the forces that come for our decency, humor, and freedom will be extolling, in beautiful smooth voices, the virtue of decency, humor, and freedom.

Imagine that the Megaphone has two dials: one controls the Intelligence of its rhetoric and the other its Volume. Ideally, the Intelligence would be set on High, and the Volume on Low—making it possible for multiple, contradictory voices to be broadcast and heard. But to the extent that the Intelligence is set on Stupid, and the Volume on Drown Out All Others, this is verging on propaganda, and we have a problem, one that works directly against the health of our democracy.

Is there an antidote?

Well, there is, but it's partial, and may not work, and isn't very exciting. Can we legislate against Stupidity? I don't think we'd want to. Freedom means we have to be free to be Stupid, and Banal, and Perverse, free to generate both *Absalom! Absalom!*, and *Swapping Pets: The Alligator Edition*. Freedom means that if some former radio DJ can wrestle his way to the top of the heap and provoke political upheavals by spouting his lame opinions and bullying his guests, he too has a right to have a breakfast cereal named after him. American creative energy has always teetered on the brink of insanity. "Rhapsody in Blue" and "The Night Chicago Died" have, alas, common DNA, the DNA for "joyfully reckless confidence."

What I propose as an antidote is simply: awareness of the Megaphonic tendency, and discussion of same. Every well-thought-out rebuttal to dogma, every scrap of intelligent logic, every absurdist reduction of some bullying stance is the antidote. Every request for the clarification of the vague, every poke at smug banality, every pen stroke in a document under revision is the antidote.

This battle, like any great moral battle, will be won, if won, not with some easy corrective tidal wave of Total Righteousness, but with small drops of specificity and aplomb and correct logic, delivered titrationally, by many of us all at once.

We have met the enemy and he is us, yes, yes, but the fact that we have recognized ourselves as the enemy indicates that we still have the ability to rise up and whip our own ass, so to speak: keep reminding ourselves that representations of the world are never the world itself. Turn that Megaphone down, and insist that what's said through it be as precise, intelligent, and humane as possible.

II

REFRAMING THE MESSAGE

WHAT THE MEDIA CAN DO

George Lakoff

George Lakoff is a cognitive linguist and the Richard and Rhoda Goldman Distinguished Professor of Cognitive Science and Linguistics at the University of California at Berkeley. He is the author of numerous books about the political uses of metaphor, including Don't Think of an Elephant.

Throughout the election, Democrats and most of the media looked upon Donald Trump as a clown, a dimwit, a mere jerk, a reality show star who did not understand the issues and who could not possibly win when he was insulting so many demographic groups. I am anything but a Trump fan, but I estimated that he would get about 47 percent of the vote. Although I was sure he wouldn't quite win, I kept warning people that he could, especially given the Democrats' failure to understand the role of conservative values and their importance to voters.

Nine months before the election I wrote about how Trump used the brains of people listening to him to his advantage. Here is a recap of how Trump does it, with examples taken from his campaign.

Unconscious thought works by certain basic mechanisms. Trump uses them instinctively to turn people's brains toward what he wants: Absolute authority, money, power, and celebrity.

The mechanisms are:

1. Repetition. Words are neurally linked to the circuits that determine their meaning. The more a word is heard, the more the circuit is activated and the stronger it gets, and so the easier it is to fire again. Trump repeats. Win. Win, Win. We're gonna win so much you'll get tired of winning.

2. Framing: Crooked Hillary. Framing Hillary as purposely and knowingly committing crimes for her own benefit, which is what a crook does. Repeating makes many people unconsciously think of her that way, even though she has always been found to have been honest and legal by thorough studies by the right-wing Benghazi committee (which found nothing) and the FBI (which found nothing to charge her with). Yet the framing worked.

    There is a common metaphor that Immorality Is Illegality, and that acting against Strict Father Morality (the only kind of morality rec-

ognized) is being immoral. Since virtually everything Hillary Clinton has ever done has violated
Strict Father Morality, that makes her immoral
to strict conservatives—which in turn makes her
a crook. The chant "Lock her up!" activates this
whole line of reasoning.

3. Well-known examples: When a well-publicized
   disaster happens, the media coverage is repeated
   over and over. Neurally, the repetition activates
   the frame-circuitry for it over and over, strength-
   ening the synapses with each repetition. Neural
   circuits with strong synapses can be activated
   more easily than those with weak synapses, and
   so the probability that they will be activated
   is higher. And so the frame is more likely to
   be activated.

   Repeated examples of shootings by Muslims,
   African Americans, and Latinos make it seem
   probable that it could happen to you—despite
   the miniscule actual probability. Trump uses
   this technique to create fear. Fear tends to activate desire for a strong strict father to protect
   you—namely, Trump.

4. Grammar: Radical Islamic terrorists: "Radical"
   puts Muslims on a linear scale and "terrorists"
   imposes a frame on the scale, suggesting that
   terrorism is built into the religion itself. The
   grammar suggests that there is something about
   Islam that has terrorism inherent in it. Imagine
   calling the Charleston gunman a "radical Republican terrorist."

Trump is aware of this to at least some extent. As he said to Tony Schwartz, the ghostwriter who wrote *The Art of the Deal* for him, "I call it truthful hyperbole. It's an innocent form of exaggeratio—and it's a very effective form of promotion."

5. Conventional metaphorical thought is inherent in our largely unconscious thought. Such normal modes of metaphorical thinking are not noticed as such. Consider Brexit, which used the metaphor of "entering" and "leaving" the EU.

There is a universal metaphor that states of being are bounded regions in space: you can enter a state, be deep in some state, and come out of that state. If you enter a café and then leave the café, you will be in the same location as before you entered.

That need not be true of states of being. But that was the metaphor used with Brexit; Britons believed that after leaving the EU, things would be as before they entered the EU. They were wrong. Things changed radically while they were in the EU.

That same metaphor is being used by Trump: Make America Great Again. Make America Safe Again. And so on. As if there was some past ideal state that we can go back to just by electing Trump.

6. There is also a metaphor that A Country Is a Person and a metonymy of the President Standing for the Country. Thus, Obama, via both meta-

phor and metonymy, can stand conceptually for America. Therefore, by saying that Obama is weak and not respected, it is communicated that America, with Obama as president, is weak and disrespected. The inference is that it is because of Obama.

The corresponding inference is that, with a strong president like Trump, the country should be strong, and via strict father reasoning, respected.

7. The country as person metaphor and the metaphor that war or conflict between countries is a fistfight between people, leads to the inference that just having a strong president will guarantee that America will win conflicts and wars. Trump will just throw knockout punches. In his acceptance speech at the convention, Trump repeatedly said that he would accomplish things that, in reality, can only be done through established government channels. After one such statement, there was a chant from the floor, "He will do it."

8. The metaphor that The Nation Is a Family was used throughout the GOP convention. We heard that strong military sons are produced by strong military fathers and that "defense of country is a family affair." From Trump's love of family and commitment to their success, we are to conclude that, as president, he will love America's citizens and be committed to the success of all.

9. There is a common metaphor that identifying with your family's national heritage makes you

a member of that nationality. Suppose your grandparents came from Italy and you identify with your Italian ancestors, you may proudly state that you are Italian. The metaphor is natural. Literally, you have been American for two generations. Trump made use of this commonplace metaphor in attacking U.S. District Court Judge Gonzalo Curiel, who is American, born and raised in the United States. Trump said that because Curiel was a Mexican, the judge would therefore hate him and rule against him in a case brought against Trump University for fraud.

10. Then there is the metaphor system used in the phrase "to call someone out." First the word "out." There is a general metaphor that Knowing Is Seeing, as in "I see what you mean." Things that are hidden inside something cannot be seen and hence not known, while things that are not hidden but out in public can be seen and hence known. To "out" someone is to make their private knowledge public. To "call someone out" is to publicly name someone's hidden misdeeds, thus allowing for public knowledge and appropriate consequences.

This is the basis for the Trumpian metaphor that Naming Is Identifying. Thus naming your enemies will allow you to identify correctly who they are, get to them, and so allow you to defeat them. Hence, just saying "radical Islamic terrorists" allows you to pick them out, get at them, and annihilate them. And conversely, if you don't say it, you won't be able to pick them out and annihilate them. Thus a failure to use those words means that you are protecting those enemies—in this case Muslims, that is, potential terrorists because of their religion.

I could go on, but I think you get the idea. Our neural minds think in certain patterns. Trump knows how to exploit them. Whatever other limitations on his knowledge, he knows a lot about using your brain against you to acquire and maintain power and money.

It is vitally important for the public to be aware of how their brains can be used against them. Can the media do such a job? There are many forces working against it.

First, there is obvious pressure on those reporting on politics in the media to assume that thought is conscious and to avoid talking about matters outside of public political discourse, that is, don't talk about things your audience can't understand.

Second, many in the media accept Enlightenment Reason. It is common for progressive pundits to quote conservative claims in conservative language and then argue against it, assuming that negating a frame will wipe it out, when instead negating a frame activates and strengthens the frame.

Third, there is the metaphor that Objectivity Is Balance, that interviews are about opinions and that opinions should be balanced.

Fourth, there are political and economic levers of power that are being used on the media. Trump is choosing the new members of the Federal Communications Commission, which has the power to take away broadcast licenses.

The Congress has the power of the purse over National Public Broadcasting and one can already see where NPR correspondents are hesitant to challenge lies. Similarly, corporate advertisers have that power over radio and TV stations, as do their corporate owners.

Fifth, there are ratings, which mean advertising money. The head of CBS, Leslie Moonves, for example, said that CBS benefitted by giving Trump free airtime during the campaign. "It may not be good for America, but it's good for CBS," he said.

Sixth, it is virtually impossible during an interview to do instant fact-checking or constantly interrupt an interviewee to confront his lies, or at least report them. It would of course lead the interviewee to refuse future interviews with that reporter or that station—or banish him or her from the White House Press Corps.

The result is media intimidation and steps toward the loss of the free press. The question is whether people in the media can join together in courage when their careers, and hence their livelihoods, are threatened.

One possibility is for journalists to use more accurate language. Take, for instance, the concept of government regulations. Regulations protect the public from harm and fraud committed by unscrupulous corporations. The Trump administration wants to get rid of "regulations." They are actually getting rid of protection. Can journalists actually say they are getting rid of "protections"—making sure to say the word "protection," and report on the harm that would be done by not protecting the public.

Can the media report on corporate poisoning of the public—through introducing lead and other cancer-causing agents into the water through fracking and various manu-facturing processes, through making food or toiletries that contain poisonous and cancer-causing ingredients, and on and on? Environmental regulations are there for a pur-pose—protection. Can the media use the words *poison* and *cancer*? The public needs to know.

Seventh, there are science-of-mind constraints. Report-ers and commentators are expected to stick to what is con-scious and contains literal meaning. But most real political discourse makes use of unconscious thought, which shapes conscious thought via framing and commonplace concep-tual metaphors, as we have seen. Can the media figure out a way to say what is in this article?

More than ever we need courage and imagination in the media. It is crucial, for the history of the country and the world, as well as the planet.

ARTISTS AND SOCIAL JUSTICE 2016–2020

Nato Thompson

Nato Thompson is an arts activist and the artistic director at Creative Time.

With the election of Donald Trump, a tangible sense of doom has permeated America, and the urgency to act, to find solace in community, or maybe even to hide, runs deep. Artists can help us with all of those reactions, and above all, they can create work that challenges the forces that brought this situation into existence and will continue operating throughout Trump's presidency.

In a perverse manner, the Trump election pointed toward a long-known truth of our social existence: culture is king. An election between two of the least loved candidates of all time, 2016's race offered a sideshow so compelling that America stared at it for a year and a half nonstop. The tabloid narrative of Trump's rise was so bizarre that not only did *The New York Times*, CNN, and every other media outlet focus on it incessantly (trapped like Buzzfeed in a constant addiction to click-bait), but so too did users at home on social media madly share articles, stoking the viral troll behavior that was perhaps the greatest cultural force in this election.

Whether it was building the wall, denigrating Islamic military families, taking jabs at POWs or grabbing women by the pussy, Trump's sheer despicability became the news. Even the offended masses seemed unable to stop following his racist, misogynistic, and erratic behavior.

This kind of cultural dynamic is emblematic of communication today. Fear, indignation, or simply taking aim at an enemy of whatever political or social stripe tends to be the emotional tone of our news. Widely shared articles say as much about a public's own sense of identity as about the content itself. And communication of the news more often than not comes out of the spirit of being against something rather than for it. No wonder both candidates were the least liked. The lesser of two evils is actually how the public votes. To put that in perspective, this election can be read as a question of anti-Hillary vs. anti-Trump.

And the feedback loop of effective, emotionally charged communication remains a critical part of the sociopolitical arena that must be challenged. One could say, "If CNN can't resist it, who can?" That work must fall to those not dependent on click-bait ratings and kneejerk emotional tactics—the artists.

First, artists must consider what it means to operate in this feedback loop of indignant communication. Take, for example, the most prevalent slogan at the widespread

post-election demonstrations in American cities: Love
Trumps Hate. The phrase is catchy in an Obama "Yes, we
can" sort of way . . . as though the world of meaning must
now be reduced to mimetic jingles; a warfare of hashtag vi-
rality. But who is the Love Trumps Hate message for? Certainly, it is written with a desire to communicate to that red
state *other*, but its ultimate goal is to comfort liberals and
reinforce the narrative that you are choosing love over hate
if you didn't vote for Trump. In a sort of a passive-aggressive
way, the message seems to want to overtly state, with clear
pride, "I am for love and some people are for hate!" Well,
okay, if it makes you feel better. But the phrase smacks of
emotionally manipulative mass identification.

But when it comes to the Trump presidency, artists
are going to have to grapple with the fact that we are not
all on the same team, for certainly events of this most recent election season have shown complex concerns around
race, gender, sexuality, and class that do not comfortably
fit within the red suburban/rural vs. blue city paradigm of
mass identification.

In 2016, cultural organizer and artist Daniel Tucker
put together a multicity and multi-artist project to speak to
some of these concerns. Titled "Organize Your Own," the
project took as its inspiration a statement from fifty years
ago that launched a subsequent organizing effort by the Student Non-Violent Coordinating Committee. SNCC's leader,
Stokely Carmichael, argued:

> One of the most disturbing things about almost all
> white supporters of the movement has been that they
> are afraid to go into their own communities—which is

where the racism exists—and work to get rid of it. They
want to run from Berkeley to tell us what to do in Mississippi; let them look instead at Berkeley... Let them go
to the suburbs and open up freedom schools for whites.

Tucker's "Organize Your Own" asked contemporary
artists, activists, and organizers to react to Carmichael's
idea that whites should be turning inward into their own
communities to organize whites against racism. Over the
next few years, I would like to see more artistic initiatives
that take up this challenge. This would mean both moving
projects toward rural and suburban areas (no small thing
considering there is little financial support for such a move)
as well as instigating projects that dig deep into the emotional and political terrain that constructs "whiteness."

We also need art to keep revealing our division in meaningful ways. When the artist Kara Walker produced her
towering, sugar-coated, sphinx-like monument, *A Subtlety*,
at the Domino Sugar Factory in 2014, this artwork amazed,
confused, inspired, outraged, and titillated a mass audience.
The work was "an Homage to the unpaid and overworked
Artisans who have refined our Sweet tastes from the cane
fields to the Kitchens of the New World on the Occasion of
the demolition of the Domino Sugar Refining Plant." Online
conversations erupted not only about the brutality of slavery
and the contemporary manifestations of racism, but perhaps, more poignantly, about the problematics of different
audiences' reception to the work. Some audiences saw the
almost tourist, selfie-taking approach that white audiences
took to the project as indicative of white culture's oblivious-
ness to the pain that the artwork evoked, for example. This

is all to say, the artwork exposed something very important: we are not on the same page.

Rather than glossing over our differences, I think they are fundamental to determining our next moves. If art has any power, it is the power of articulating what it means to feel in this world. It is embodied, wild, fearful, and desirous. It is somatic and social. As we head into this turbulent period in American history, we must also acknowledge the nuances of our political concerns so that we don't gloss over them. If click-bait fueled by indignance cannot capture that nuance, then our president's unhinged (and "post-truth") tweets certainly cannot capture it. Only artists aware of our deep divisions, and willing to explore them, truly can. And so, artists will not only be at the forefront of our resistance—they may even have to succeed where journalists have failed. And, like many journalists, many artists will also become casualties.

The capacity to produce a more nuanced discussion that cuts across ideology, geography, and political party will be as essential as ever. Every political party is racist, patriarchal, and capitalist. Power moves across all of us fluidly. Whether artists address inequities in the cities or even dare to take the trains toward the land of strip malls, churches, and box stores, their work must reject the kneejerk reaction to reject other voices—and instead take into account the serious complexities of what makes people who they are.

Theresa Rose contributed writing to this piece.

CODA

NONE OF THE OLD RULES APPLY

TRAVELS THROUGH POST-ELECTION AMERICA

Dave Eggers

*Dave Eggers is the author of numerous novels,
the publisher of* McSweeney's, *and an education
activist whose organizing includes cofounding
the 826 Valencia literacy project.*

The word *surreal* is overused and often wrongly used, but
in the case of the *Washington Post* Election Night Live party,
the word was apt. First of all, it was a disco. There was a DJ
playing a frenetic mix of contemporary Top 40 and point-
edly apropos songs, such as Pat Benatar's "Hit Me With
Your Best Shot" ("You're a real tough cookie with a long history . . ."). Behind the DJ there were dozens of screens showing various television networks' coverage of the election. The
screens were so bright and so huge, and the colors so pri-

mary and vivid, that the experience was like being trapped inside an enormous jar of jelly beans.

Women dressed like Vegas showgirls made their way through the crowd with towering tiered hats adorned with chocolates from one of the evening's sponsors. The chocolates, round and the size of strawberries, were offered in pairs, enclosed in loose plastic sacks—a bizarre but perhaps intentionally lewd optic? The bartenders were setting out Campari Americanos by the dozens. The food was by chefs José Andrés and the brothers Voltaggio. *The Washington Post* has a right to celebrate—the paper is thriving and its political coverage extraordinary—but this felt like Rome before the fall.

At some point early on, the music was turned down for twenty minutes so Karen Attiah of the *Post* could moderate a live conversation between the current German ambassador, Peter Wittig, and former Mexican ambassador Arturo Sarukhan. The talk was serious and enlightening, but the ambassadors seemed baffled by the nightclub atmosphere, and besides, few people were listening. The party was about the party.

And everyone expected Hillary Clinton to win. The attendees were largely Washington insiders—lobbyists, staffers, legislative aides, pundits, and producers. Most were liberal and most were confident. The night's only potential for suspense centered around whether or not Clinton would take some of the toss-up states, like Florida and North Carolina. When she was declared the winner—which was expected before the party's scheduled end time of ten o'clock—there would be talk of who would be appointed what, with a not-insignificant portion of the partygoers in line for positions in the new administration.

Thus the mood was ebullient at seven o'clock, when the event started, and was electric by eight. Kentucky and Indiana were announced for Donald Trump and that news was met with a shrug. More scantily clad women walked through the rooms serving hors d'oeuvres, and soon there were at least three showgirls wearing hats of towering testicle-chocolates. Young Washingtonians swayed to the music. Drinks were set under chairs and spilled. A young girl in a beautiful party dress walked through the drunken partygoers looking for her parents.

Then nine o'clock came around and the party began to turn. Most of the states thus far had gone for Trump. None of these victories was unexpected, but the reddening of the national map was disheartening, and the margins in those states were often greater than expected. He took Texas, North Dakota, Kansas, Mississippi. Not a problem for the crowd, but by 9:30, people were panicking. Trump was leading in Florida and North Carolina. Nate Silver, the statistics shaman who had been roundly criticized for overestimating Trump's chances, now posted that a Trump victory was likely. Ohio was in the bag, Pennsylvania was trending toward him, and it looked like he could win Wisconsin and Michigan. A hundred guests turned their attention from the big screens to their little screens. They paced and made calls. The party emptied and we all spilled into the streets. Beyond *The Washington Post* building and beyond D.C., the country had been swamped by a white tsunami few saw coming.

For a few hours, the city had the feeling of a disaster movie. People scurried this way and that. Some wandered around dazed. Following the returns, we travelled from restaurant to bar to home, and the Somali and Ethiopian cabbies were stunned, worried less about Trump than about the prospect of Rudy Giuliani serving in the cabinet in any capacity. We all talked about where we will move: Belize; New Zealand; Canada. We no longer knew our own country. In Columbia Heights, when the election was settled, a young woman biking up the hill stopped, threw her bike into the middle of the road, sat on a curb and began weeping. "No no no no," she wailed.

The omens were there if you looked. A month before the election, I'd driven from Pittsburgh to the Philadelphia suburbs and saw nothing but Trump/Pence signs. In three days I covered about 1,200 miles of back roads and highway—some of the prettiest country you can find on this continent—and saw not one sign, large or small, in support of Clinton. The only time any mention of her was made at all was on an enormous billboard bearing her face with a Pinocchio nose.

I did see Confederate flags. James Carville, the political strategist, recently quipped that Pennsylvania is Pittsburgh and Philadelphia with Alabama in between, and there is some truth to that. There are a lot of men in camouflage jackets. There are a lot of men out of work. When you stop at gas stations, the magazine sections are overwhelmed by periodicals devoted to guns, hunting, and survival. Then there are the tidy farms and rolling hills, the equestrian centers with their white fences, the wide swaths of Amish and Mennonites and Quakers.

I was in rural Pennsylvania to see the United 93 National Memorial in Shanksville—a monument to the forty passengers and crew who died in a windswept field on 9/11. The day I visited was bright and clear. The surrounding country was alive with autumn colors and, far on distant ridgelines, white windmills turned slowly. Just off the parking lot, a park ranger in forest green was standing before a diverse group of middle school students, admonishing them.

"Boys and girls. Boys and girls," he said. "You're standing here where people died. There are still human remains here. You're goofing around and laughing, and I shouldn't have to tell you to be respectful. They deserve that." They quieted for a moment before one of the boys nudged another, and the giggling began again.

The memorial is beautifully constructed and devastating in its emotional punch. Visitors can walk the flight path of the plane, a gently sloping route down to the crash site, which is separated from the footpath by a low wall. "It's a grave," another ranger explained. "So we don't walk there." Higher on the hill, there is an indoor visitor center that recreates every moment of the day in excruciating detail. There are video loops of the Twin Towers being destroyed, fragments of the plane, pictures and bios of every passenger, details about the calls they made from the plane once they knew they would die. It is shattering.

Leaving the museum, a man in front of me, young and built like a weightlifter, couldn't push the door open. I reached over him to help and he turned to thank me. His face was soaked with tears. I got into my car, shaken but heartened by the courage of the forty humans who had realized what was happening—that they were passengers on a missile headed for the White House or Capitol building—and had sacrificed their lives to save untold numbers in Washington,

D.C. The American passengers of United 93 were from thirty-five different cities in eleven different states, but they died together to save the capital from incalculable loss of lives and what might have been a crippling blow to the nation's psyche.

I left the memorial and turned on to a two-lane road, part of the Lincoln Highway that runs through the state—part of the first coast-to-coast highway in the United States. Just beyond a sign advertising home-grown sweet corn, there was a residential home, the first house anyone might encounter when leaving the United Memorial, and on this home, there is a vast Confederate flag draped over the front porch.

It's important to note that this was the Lincoln Highway. And that the Civil War ended 160 years ago. And that Pennsylvania was not a state in the Confederacy. So to see this, an enormous Confederate flag in a Union state, a mile from a symbol of national tragedy and shared sacrifice, was an indicator that there was something very unusual in the mood of the country. Ancient hatreds had resurfaced. Strange alliances had been formed. None of the old rules applied.

Steven McManus has come out of the closet twice. First as a gay man, then as a Trump supporter. We were sitting at a coffeeshop in Detroit's Eastern Market neighborhood, and McManus was almost vibrating. This was two days after Trump's election, and McManus was elated—about the victory, yes, but more personally, about the fact that after Trump's election, he'd had the courage to post a message on social media declaring his support of the president-elect.

"I lived a lot of my life as a closeted guy," McManus said, "and the liberation I felt as a man coming out was similar to how I felt coming out for Trump. You really truly think you're the only one who has these feelings. It's liberating. I felt it was time to come out again."

McManus is a thin man in his late thirties, bald and be-spectacled, with a close-cropped beard. He grew up in the part of the Detroit suburbs known as Downriver. Many of the area's residents had come from the American South in the 1940s to work in the auto factories, and the area still retains a southern feel. His father was a salesman who brokered space on trucking lines. Looking back on it now, McManus appreciated the fact that his parents could raise five children on one salesman's salary. But then came the NAFTA and the gutting of much of the Detroit auto manufacturing base. McManus watched as Detroit and Flint hollowed out and caved in.

"Trump was the only candidate talking about the trade imbalance," McManus said. "Being a businessman, a successful businessman, he understood why business decision-makers, at the highest levels of their companies, move their production overseas." McManus was angry when auto companies, after receiving bailouts from the U.S. government in 2009, continued to move production to Mexico. "In Detroit, we gave America the middle class. But this is now a false economy. The housing market is decimated, and the middle class is shrinking. I want someone to shake it up. Let's move the whole country forward."

McManus is not blind to the rareness of an openly gay man supporting Trump. "But I don't have to vote a certain way based on my sexuality. In my mind we've moved beyond having to vote Democrat just because you're gay." And he's not worried about a reversal of the hard-fought right to marriage gays just achieved. "We've got our rights now," he said. "It's settled." McManus and his husband got married three years ago in New York, before the supreme court decision legalized gay marriage nationwide, and it was in his new place of domestic tranquillity that McManus watched the Republican national convention. Two moments affected him profoundly. First was the appearance of Peter Thiel, the former CEO of PayPal, who was given a prime speaker's spot and said from the stage, "Every American has a unique identity. I am proud to be gay. I am proud to be a Republican. But most of all, I am proud to be an American."

McManus was moved then, but he was even more affected by an unscripted part of Trump's speech. "It was shortly after the Orlando massacre, and for the first time in my life, a Republican candidate for president said things like, 'forty-nine wonderful Americans,' or 'beautiful Americans' or whatever he said, 'were savagely murdered.' And he said, 'I will protect gay and lesbian individuals.' Some people at the convention cheered and some people didn't cheer. And then Trump said, off the cuff and off the teleprompter, he said, 'For those of you who cheered, I thank you.' And I cried. I cried."

McManus's husband works for the army, as an IT specialist, and they both became bothered by Clinton's e-mail setup. "If my husband had done the same thing, he'd be fired. And it's pretty hard to get fired from a government job." McManus began to follow Trump more closely, and found that he was agreeing with most of his positions on

trade, immigration, and national security. "I began to realize
that I'm more conservative than I thought." But he couldn't
reveal this. He lives in Detroit, a liberal city, and works in
the restaurant industry in town, where left-leaning politics
dominate. But after coming out as a Trump supporter, he
is finding himself emboldened. The day after the election,
McManus saw his doctor, who is Muslim, and he mentioned
that he'd voted for Trump.

"I just wanted to get it off my chest. I was feeling a little . . ." McManus sits up in his chair, to indicate the new confidence he felt that day. "I told him, I came out as a Trump
supporter today. And he went off for fifteen minutes—to
the point where I almost walked out. He was impassioned
about how he felt that Trump was disenfranchising Muslim
Americans. But our present state of terrorism does have a religious undertone to it. Finally I managed to get something
off my chest. I can't remember who said this to me, either
my husband or my ex, but I said to my doctor, 'You know,
it wasn't a group of Catholic nuns that flew planes into the
World Trade Center.'"

Later that night in Detroit, I ran into Rob Mickey, a professor
of political science. He grew up in Texas, but has spent about
ten years teaching at the University of Michigan in Ann Ar-
bor. We were at a party benefiting an educational nonprofit.
Doing something concrete and positive felt good, and being around kids felt good, but everyone was exhausted—no
one had slept since the election—and thirty seconds into
every conversation it turned to Trump, Clinton, what had

gone wrong and what would happen next. One of the event's attendees had been living in a central American cloud forest for years, and there was much talk about following her down there.

I told Mickey about McManus, and to him, the story of the gay Trump supporter was both surprising and unsurprising. Everything about 2016 was upside down. Parts of Michigan who had voted twice for Obama had turned to Trump. Rob and his wife Jenny had gone canvassing for Clinton on the Sunday before the election, and the reception they received was not warm.

"I would say it was hostile," he said.

They had gone to Milan, Michigan, an overwhelmingly white town fifty miles southwest of Detroit. "It's spelled like the Italian town, but pronounced *MY-lan*," Rob pointed out. The Clinton campaign had given Rob and Jenny a list of names and addresses of white working-class residents who had registered as Democrats but were labeled "sporadic voters." Milan had voted for Obama in 2008 and 2012, and winning towns such as Milan was key to delivering a Clinton victory in Michigan.

The homes they visited were run-down, with "NO SOLICITING" placards on every door. They saw no Clinton signs on anyone's lawn. There were Trump signs scattered around town, but most of the residents they met were disgusted by the entire election.

"One woman said, 'I don't want to have nothing to do with that,'" Mickey recalled. "Another said, 'I hate them both, including that guy of yours.' When I pointed out that our candidate was a woman, she said, 'Whatever,' and slammed the door."

One house with a Bernie Sanders sign on the lawn looked promising. Mickey knocked on the door. A white man with a U.S. ARMY shirt answered. He was missing an arm. Mickey introduced himself as a Clinton canvasser, and told the man he had supported Sanders, too, during the primary. "That's great," the man said, and closed the door.

"The people we met that day were straight out of central casting, if you were making a movie about the disaffected white working class," Mickey said. "Between fifty-five and sixty-five, without college degrees. You could see that Lena Dunham and Katy Perry were not going to do anything to form a bridge to these people. If I hadn't read any polls, and I was basing it just on the people I met, I would have thought, boy, Clinton's going to get wiped out."

It was different in 2008. Knowing that Michigan was securely in Obama's column and Ohio was on the bubble, Rob and Jenny went to Toledo to knock on doors in trailer parks and housing projects. Foreclosure signs were common. When they introduced themselves as canvassers for Obama, the residents, all of them white, were welcoming and chatty. "The interactions were long," Mickey said. "The people were worried and they wanted to talk." Ohio's eighteen electoral votes went to Obama in 2008 and 2012.

"This campaign wore a lot of people down," Mickey said. "The state was bombarded by pro-Clinton ads, but she failed to offer any sustained and coherent economic message. She said, 'I'm not crazy' and 'I'm not a sexist racist pig,' but for working-class whites that's not enough. I would say that of the people who slammed their doors on me, most of them didn't vote for either candidate."

In fact, an unprecedented number of Michigan voters

cast ballots without choosing either Clinton or Trump. This kind of voting happens every election—where voters make their preferences known down ballot but don't mark anyone for president—but never in such numbers. In 2012, there were 50,000 Michigan voters who declined to choose any presidential candidate. In 2016, there were 110,000.

Clinton lost Michigan by 13,107 votes.

The week after the election, the business of the United States went on. Schools and banks were open. The stock market plummeted and rose to a new high. Commuters commuted, and I was headed from Detroit to Kentucky. All of this was travel planned months before, and none of it had anything to do with the election, but it felt like I was making my way, intentionally, into the heart of Trump country.

At the Detroit airport it was impossible not to feel the tragedy of Tuesday as having realigned our relationships with each other. Because the voting had split so dramatically along racial lines, how could an African American or Latino pass a white person on the street, or at baggage claim, and not wonder, "Which side are you on?"

The emergence of safety pins to symbolize support for Clinton (and equality and inclusion) was inevitable—it fulfilled a need, particularly on the part of white Americans, to signal where they stand. Otherwise, all iconography is subject to misinterpretation. At the airport, I found an older white man staring at me. His eyes narrowed to slits. I was baffled until I realized he was looking at my baseball hat, which bore the logo and name of a Costa Rican beer called

Imperial. Was this man a Clinton supporter who suspected me of being a white nationalist? Was the word Imperial sending a Ku Klux Klan/Third Reich signal to him?

Anyway, I was in the wrong terminal. I was in danger of missing a flight to Louisville, so I left and poked my head into a Hertz bus and asked the driver if he would be stopping near Delta anytime soon. He paused for a moment.

"Yeah, I'll take you," he said.

His name was Carl. He was a lanky African American man in his sixties, and we rode alone, just me and him in this enormous bus, for a time. He asked how I was doing. I told him I was terrible. I *was* feeling terrible, but I also wanted him to know which side I was on. He laughed.

"Yeah, I was surprised on Tuesday, too," he said. "But I almost feel sorry for Trump. I don't think he thought he'd actually win. You see him sitting next to Obama at the Oval Office? He looked like a child."

In Louisville, three days after the election, I sat with thirty-two students at Fern Creek High School. This was supposed to be a regular classroom visit by someone passing through, but the atmosphere was different now. The students at Fern Creek are from twenty-eight countries. They speak forty-one languages. There are refugees from Syria, South Sudan, and the Democratic Republic of Congo. We sat in an oval and ate samosas. Nepalese samosas, I was told. Three of the students in the class were from Nepal, and had a particular recipe. The food was extraordinary.

I told these students, three girls still learning English,

that I'd always wanted to go to Nepal, and asked them to write down some places they'd recommend. They wrote "Jhapa, Damak (Refugee camp)." They were from Bhutan and had grown up in a UNHCR camp in eastern Nepal. A young man to my left had come from Iraq two years earlier.

Their teachers, Joseph Franzen and Brent Peters, guided the conversation through topics of creativity, social justice, and empathy. The students were without exception thoughtful, attentive, and respectful of each other's opinions. Every time a student finished a statement, the rest of the class snapped, Beat-style, in appreciation. We didn't talk politics. For the time being, the students had had enough of politics. The day after the election, they'd had a charged discussion about the results, and, still feeling raw, they had written about the discussion the next day.

The thing I didn't say yesterday was that Muslims scare me. The thing with Isis is out of control and I don't trust them at all and I don't get why Mexicans can't take the test to become legal? Are they lazy?

The election didn't really bother me even with the outcome, I didn't support Trump. The main reason I cared about Clinton winning was 'cause I didn't want my family to be affected. My mom is gay and married to a woman.

As a Muslim female in high school it's hard to deal with this and let it sink in. But I know Trump doesn't have full power of his actions. So I feel like even if he's president, everything will be the same.

I was downright disappointed in the country. Because Trump won, racism, sexism, misogyny and xenophobia won. It goes to show what our country values now. Either this is what we value, or this is what the majority is OK with.

I feel like everything said yesterday doesn't even matter anymore. We as American citizens can't change what's been decided. Not everybody gets what they want. That's what life is. Trump will be our new president and we can't change that. *We* need to make America great again, *not* Trump. That's our job as people.

I think Trump and Hillary are both crazy and I'm kind of eager to see how trump runs this b---h.

And so we see how differently we express ourselves on paper. The students, sitting in their oval with the smell of Nepalese samosas filling the room, were unfailingly kind to each other. But on paper, other selves were unleashed. Despite the many international students, the school's population is mostly American born, 48 percent white and 38 percent black, and it was easy to see how Trump could bring dormant grievances to the fore, could give license to reactionary theories and kneejerk assumptions. The students had witnessed eight years of exquisite presidential self-control and dignity, and now there would be a seventy-year-old man in the White House whose feelings were easily hurt, who called people names, and who tweeted his complaints at all hours, with rampant misspellings and exclamation marks. Our only hope will be that the 100 million or so young people in American schools behave better than the president. A president who has not read a book since he was last required to. Think of it.

After the class, a tall African American student named Devin approached me. He'd introduced himself before the class, and had asked some very sophisticated questions about using imagery to convey meaning in his poetry. He was a wide receiver on the school's football team, he said, but he was also a writer. He handed me a loose-leaf piece of paper, and on it was a prose-poem he wanted me to look at.

> We sat on top of my house, laying back, looking at the stars, the stars shining, waving back at us. They told us hello. Time froze. I turned my head to look at you. Still fixated on the stars, you paid me no mind. I studied you. This was the true face of beauty. Your royal blue eyes, the brown polka dots on your face. Your smile making the moon envious because it could not compare in light. I reached out to grab your hand. You turned your eyes to look at me. Our hands intersected and we both smiled. I told you you were beautiful.

Below the piece, Devin wrote, in red ink, "Do I have something here? Should I continue?"

That night in Louisville there was another benefit event, this one for an organization called Teach Kentucky, which recruits high-achieving college graduates to come to the state to teach in the public schools. Joe Franzen and Brent Peters are among Teach Kentucky's recruits, and if they are any indication of the quality of humans the organization is attracting, the program is a runaway success.

At the event, Franzen and Peters spoke about their craft, and about making sure their students felt they had a place at the table. There was much talk about their classrooms as families, of meals shared by all, of mutual respect. It was very calm and heartening, but there was also a moment where the audience was encouraged to let out a primal scream (my idea, I admit it), and 200 people did that, screamed, exorcising our election-week demons. Later on, Jim James—Louisville resident and leader of the rock band My Morning Jacket— performed a medley of songs, from Leonard Cohen to "All You Need Is Love" and "Blowin' in the Wind." And then everyone got drunk.

There was good bourbon. It was called brown water by the locals, and after stomachs were full, we all vacillated between despair and measured hope. But the questions loomed over the night like the shadow of a Nazi zeppelin. Would he really try to build a wall? Would he really try to exclude all Muslims? Would he actually appoint a white nationalist as his chief of staff? And did 42 percent of American women really vote for a man who threatened to overturn *Roe v. Wade* and who bragged about grabbing them by the pussy? Did the white working class really elect a man whose most famous catchphrase was "You're fired"? Like a teenager with poor self-esteem, the American people had chosen the flashy and abusive boyfriend over the steady, boring one. *We've had enough decency for one decade*, the electorate decided. *Give us chaos.*

•   •   •

It is not easy to get a ticket to the Smithsonian's National Museum of African American History and Culture. This is the newest museum on the National Mall in Washington, D.C., and its design, by the Ghanaian-British architect David Adjaye, is so successful, at once immediately iconic and bold but also somehow blending into the low-slung surrounding architecture, that it has become the most talked-about building in the United States.

Admission is free, but there is a six-month wait for passes, and the passes are timed. If you get a pass, you must enter at the assigned hour or wait another six months. I had gotten such a timed pass, and it so happened that the pass was for the day after the election. That morning, I had the choice between staying in bed, forgoing my one chance at seeing the building in 2016, or rising on three hours' sleep and keeping the appointment. Like millions of others, I did not want the day to begin. If I woke up, I would check the news, and if I checked the news, there would be confirmation of what I had remembered foggily from the night before—that the people of America had elected a reality television host as their president. I closed my eyes, wanting sleep.

Then I remembered the Gazans.

Back in April, I had been in the Gaza Strip and had met a married couple, Mahmoud and Miriam, journalists and activists who badly wanted to leave Gaza. I had e-introduced them to an asylum lawyer in San Francisco, but from 7,000 miles away, she couldn't do much to help. The impossible thing was that they actually had a visa. A real visa issued by the American State Department. All they had to do was get out of Gaza. But permissions were needed from the Israelis or Egyptians, and they were having no luck with either. Finally, one day in October, an e-mail arrived. Mahmoud and Miriam were in Brooklyn. They'd bribed an Egyptian guard at the Rafah gate and had made their way on a fourteen-hour journey through Sinai.

So on a lark I told them to meet me in D.C. Frederick Douglass had said, after all, that every American should visit the nation's capital at least once. And given they would soon be Americans, wouldn't it be good to do that duty right away, and do it the day after the first woman had been elected president? (We had made the plans a week before.)

So they had planned to meet me at this museum celebrating African American history in the shadow of the obelisk dedicated to George Washington, great man and also slave owner. The morning was clear and cool. A small line had formed outside the museum before the doors were to open. I looked around and didn't see them. Then I did.

They were aglow. They'd spent their lives in an open-air prison of 141 square miles, and now they were here. They could move about freely, could decide one day to go to the capital of the United States and be there a few hours later. No checkpoints, no bribes, no Hamas secret police. I'd seen Miriam suffer in Gaza because she refused to wear the hijab and favored western clothes. In Gaza City, she was yelled at, cursed. "I hope your parents are proud!" people yelled to her. Now she was herself, uncovered, dressing as she chose. Her smile was incandescent.

"I'm so sorry," I said. I was apologizing for what we'd done the day before. Electing the man who wanted to ban all Muslims from entering the country. The man who might bring Giuliani into a seat of unspeakable power. This could mean terrible things for Palestinians. There was already talk of the end of the two-state solution. Netanyahu, it was assumed, had danced all night.

"It's OK," they said.

They handed me a gift. It was a piece of the Gaza City airport. The airport had been destroyed by Israel in 2002. The piece they'd brought me was tiled; it looked like part of the airport bathroom. I thanked them, put the chunk of concrete in my bag, and we wondered aloud whether the security check at the museum would object to the entry of a shard of Gazan airport. We passed through the doors, and I was allowed to keep my bag with me, so we three, and part of the Gaza City airport, made our way through the museum's halls. It was glorious of course, and altogether too much to take in in one day. We ate in the basement cafeteria, and talked about what was next. They would need an asylum lawyer, and fast. Ninety days, and then anything could happen.

"Don't worry," Mahmoud said.

The Gazan asylum seekers were telling me not to worry.

But I was worried. Worried enough to change their names in this piece. They aren't Mahmoud and Miriam. We are entering an era where uniquely vindictive men will have uniquely awesome power. Dark forces have already been unleashed and terrible plans are being made. On December 3, the Ku Klux Klan are holding their largest public rally in years, to celebrate Trump's victory, which they claim as their own. I also changed Steven McManus's name. I worried for him, as well.

You should be worried, too. George W. Bush, a man of comparative calm and measured intellect, started two foreign wars and cratered the world economy. Trump is far more reckless.

We are speeding toward a dark corridor, my friends. Keep your eyes open, your hearts stout, and be ready for the fight.

The publishers wish to thank Gloria Jacobs, Barbara Radnofsky, and Thomas Dunne for their assistance on this project.